Honestly, I am not sure if the importance of Chet Bowers' new book on the Digital Revolution can be overestimated. I say this for two reasons. First, Chet Bowers is one of the very few original thinkers we have around; his approach and understanding is quite unlike what you can read elsewhere. Second, our infatuation with progress and in particular computer technology and the internet has totally blinded us against the threat this wholesale digital revolution is posing for our democracy and indeed our very survival. Chet Bowers is eloquently providing the much needed analysis to understand what is really going on.

Rolf Jucker, Director of SILVIVA, Swiss Foundation for Experiential Environmental Education, Switzerland

In the era of systems, beyond the era of tools, we are becoming merely sub-systems, as Ivan Illich timely warned. This very pertinent book brings at a deeper level Chet Bowers' critical analysis of the digital age and its real and symbolic impact on education and our daily lives. It is an urgent call for austerity in the use of tools like the internet, in order to protect personal relatedness, conviviality, local cultural contexts, and even Mother Earth. This is not another NeoLuddite manifesto but a pertinent call to reclaim common sense.

Gustavo Esteva, Activist, Oaxaca, Mexico

Few societies have demonstrated either much foresight or skill when confronted with new and potentially disruptive technologies. Who would have imagined for example, the impact of computers on commerce, manufacturing, finance, mail delivery, education, journalism, entertainment, surveillance, or simple patterns of human interaction, just thirty years ago? Chet Bowers has been attempting to direct our attention to the consequences of the digitalization of the world for much of this time. The issues he raises in this volume deserve widespread discussion as humanity attempts to learn how to live well and humanely with what may well be the most powerful tools ever invented by our species.

Gregory Smith, Lewis and Clark College, USA

Bowers has for decades been a brilliant writer on how the ecological crisis permeates education and our western society. In this important book on the digital revolution, he shows clearly what the internet still cannot do in terms of face to face democracy and the pivotal need to revitalize the world's cultural commons. It helps us see what lacks in our ever more complicated world of digits and what is needed to lay the groundwork for reconnecting to the diversity of ecological, cultural, and moral lives that give sustenance to the meaning of *glocal* sustainability and solidarity.

Per Ingvar Haukeland, Director of Centre for Nature and Culture-Based Innovation, Telemark Research Institute, Norway

In contrast to such popular educational slogans as 'mobile learning' and 'Internet democracy,' this book not only provides a critical analysis of how the digital revolution is bypassing the democratic process, but also argues that the road to a sustainable future requires revitalizing traditions of wisdom and the cultural commons that are passed forward through face to face and mentoring relationships. This book challenges the current efforts to reduce human experience to what can be digitized and stored in the cloud.

Chun Ping Wang, Dean of Center for Teacher Education & Careers Service, National Taipei University of Education, Taiwan

DIGITAL DETACHMENT

The digital revolution is changing the world in ecologically unsustainable ways: (1) it increases the economic and political power of the elites controlling and interpreting the data; (2) it is based on the deep assumptions of market liberalism that do not recognize environmental limits; (3) it undermines face-to-face and context-specific forms of knowledge; (4) it undermines awareness of the meta-phorical nature of language; (5) its promoters are driven by the myth of progress and thus ignore important cultural traditions of the cultural commons that are being lost; and (6) it both bypasses the democratic process and colonizes other cultures. This book provides an in-depth examination of these phenomena and connects them to questions of educational reform in the US and beyond.

Chet Bowers is a semi-retired university professor who has written 23 books that examine the linguistic/cultural roots of the ecological crisis—and their implications for reforming universities and public schools. He has been an invited speaker at 40 foreign and 42 American universities.

DIGITAL DETACHMENT

How Computer Culture
Undermines Democracy

Chet Bowers

Routledge
Taylor & Francis Group

NEW YORK AND LONDON

First published 2016
by Routledge
711 Third Avenue, New York, NY 10017

and by Routledge
2 Park Square, Milton Park, Abingdon, Oxon OX14 4RN

Routledge is an imprint of the Taylor & Francis Group, an informa business

British Library Cataloguing in Publication Data
A catalogue record for this book is available from the British Library

Library of Congress Cataloging in Publication Data
Names: Bowers, C. A., author.
    Title: Digital detachment : how computer culture undermines democracy /
Chet Bowers.
    Description: New York, NY : Routledge, 2016. | Includes bibliographical
references.
    Identifiers: LCCN 2015034346| ISBN 9781138186842 (hardback) | ISBN
9781138186866 (pbk.) | ISBN 9781315643540 (e-book)
    Subjects: LCSH: Democracy. | Information society–Political aspects. |
Internet–Political aspects. | Information technology–Political aspects.
    Classification: LCC JC423 .B759 2016 | DDC 303.48/33–dc23
LC record available at http://lccn.loc.gov/2015034346

ISBN: 978-1-138-18684-2 (hbk)
ISBN: 978-1-138-18686-6 (pbk)
ISBN: 978-1-315-64354-0 (ebk)

Typeset in Bembo
by Taylor & Francis Books

Printed and bound in the United States of America by Publishers Graphics,
LLC on sustainably sourced paper.

In memory of Douglas Tompkins—a force for nature and ecological intelligence

CONTENTS

CONTRIBUTORS

Chet Bowers is a semi-retired university professor who has written 23 books that examine the linguistic/cultural roots of the ecological crisis—and their implications for reforming universities and public schools. He has been an invited speaker at 40 foreign and 42 American universities.

Joseph Progler has worked as a journalist on the Muslim world, and has been an invited speaker at schools, universities, and NGOs in Malaysia, Pakistan, Jordan, Palestine, and Turkey. He helped develop a degree program in International Studies at Zayed University in Dubai, and has lectured and taught courses in Iran, including at the University of Medical Sciences in Isfahan, Alzahrah University in Tehran, and the University of Religions and Denominations in Qom. The author of *Books for Critical Consciousness* and *Encountering Islam*, he currently teaches humanities at Ritsumeikan Asia Pacific University in Japan.

Azra Kianinejad has worked as an editor and researcher in Iran, at the Islamic Thought Foundation and Islamic Republic of Iran Broadcasting, has taught at Azad University in Tehran and the School of Islamic Arts in Qom, and has been an invited speaker at the Iranian Society for eLearning. The author of articles on education and society, she currently teaches comparative religions at Ritsumeikan Asia Pacific University in Japan.

PREFACE

This book challenges the continuing optimism that the Internet will serve as the vehicle for revitalizing the democratic process. Seemingly unlimited access to information, massive amounts of data on every aspect of social life and on the deepening ecological crisis, the sharing of ideas by both highly intelligent individuals as well as by extremists, and the ease with which everyone can launch her/his own ideas into cyberspace suggests we are on the cusp of a radical transformation that leads to a genuinely democratic society. The widespread use of surveillance technologies, and the governmental agencies and cowboy capitalists that benefit from them, have taken some of the wind out of this optimism. It now turns out that the unrelenting quest to develop new markets and corporate profits rather than revitalizing democracy are the primary goals of the technology giants such as Google, Microsoft, Facebook, Apple, AT &T, and Amazon.

Democracy is one of the god-words, along with "freedom" and "progress," that everyone supports even as many of them spread disinformation and mistrust of everyone who does not share their ideas. It would be easy to claim that the Internet, in facilitating the spread of polarizing ideas, is putting the country on the slippery slope leading to an anti-democratic future. The issues I examine in this book move the discussion of the disconnects between the Internet and democracy to a deeper level that even challenges the assumptions of progressive and social justice thinkers. This deeper level is based on the recognition that the digital revolution continues to rely upon age-old languaging processes and thus cannot escape reproducing the misconceptions and silences of earlier eras. These misconceptions and silences are currently being reproduced in the thinking of computer futurist writers such as Ray Kurzweil, Eric Schmidt, and Peter Diamandis who mistakenly promote the digital revolution as an inherently progressive and modernizing technology. Their writings are noteworthy for their lack of understanding of the connections between democracy and the ability of people to debate the merits of the lived traditions that should be overturned and those that need to be intergenerationally renewed.

What is ignored by computer futurist writers, computer scientists focused on creating new digital technologies, software programmers, educators socializing students to think in the abstract world of the Internet, and hackers is that the traditions reenacted in everyday life are the primary basis of local democratic decision making. Personal interests in the economics of the household and increasing uncertainties about being displaced by computer-driven automation, as well as the interplay between political and moral issues encountered in everyday life, are largely marginalized by the abstract nature of the data and information acquired through computer-mediated thinking and communication. In short, the promoters of the digital revolution are not aware they are perpetuating in the name of progress the abstract patterns of thinking that have served the interests of ideological and economic elites over the last four hundred or so years. These elites continue to promote a consumer-dependent lifestyle that is contributing to the loss of habitats, species, and changes in the chemistry of the world's oceans. That the elites now promoting the digital revolution were educated in the West's best educational institutions raises the question whether universities are capable of reforming themselves, or if the paradigm shift necessary for living ecologically sustainable lifestyles will come from the grass roots awakening to the importance of the localism movement spreading around the world.

Thus, one of the primary foci of the book is the cultural and linguistic issues not addressed in the education of the highly motivated army of innovators and promoters of the digital revolution. These true believers unknowingly have adopted the abstract agenda first promoted by René Descartes (1596–1650) and John Locke (1632–1704): namely, that intelligence should not be constrained by a knowledge of one's cultural traditions, especially the traditions that are more community-centered and less destructive of the natural environment. The importance of acquiring knowledge of the traditions of other cultures had no relevance for these ethnocentric thinkers. Indeed, what was missing in their education is now being reproduced in the education of the current generation that is becoming increasingly dependent upon the digital technologies now producing great wealth for the technological elites promoting a dangerously narrow understanding of the connections between knowledge and empowerment. Abstract data is becoming the new basis of intelligence in a connected, individually centered world that supposedly transcends cultural boundaries and alternative ways of knowing.

It is the long-standing failure to understand the cultural and linguistic limitations of Internet technologies that lead computer scientists, and their many followers, to mis-educate the public into thinking that data and information should be the primary basis for making democratic decisions about the mal-distribution of wealth, the now life-altering ecological crisis, and what the nation's social priorities should be. What is being overlooked as the digital revolution enables people to carry out many previously difficult tasks and to achieve higher levels of efficiency and profits is that the highly specialized and narrow education of the computer scientists has left them without a knowledge of the cultures into which their technologies are introduced. The acclaim they receive from the business community and cowboy capitalists, environmental scientists, educators, and the general public seeking to live in a more connected world reinforces the long held cultural assumption that social progress is achieved primarily through technological innovations. Their libertarian ideology, which is based on abstract theory totally devoid of any consideration of cultural differences, further blinds them from considering the differences in cultural ways of knowing—including whether the cultural assumptions they take for granted contribute to an ecologically unsustainable future.

Overlooked by the computer scientists are the deep cultural assumptions promoted by the digital revolution. Unfortunately, this has not diminished public support of how they are transforming the world. A recent Pew Internet Research Project found that 85 percent of the computer-using public eagerly awaits the emerging totally connected world now referred to as the Internet/Cloud of Things. With estimates of 20 to 25 billion data and wireless connection devices to be used in homes, businesses, and in personal activities by 2025, the amount of data will be so overwhelming that few people will have the time and energy to reflect on the deep cultural assumptions that have transformed their world into one of total surveillance. Ironically, personal efforts to use social networks to ensure being watched by the widest possible audience suggest that the regression into the culture of narcissism is now being taken as a sign of success and well-being.

While the digital technologies appear to be new, they are based on the same deep cultural assumptions that underlie the industrial/consumer-dependent culture that is overshooting the sustaining capacity of the Earth's natural systems. These centuries-old Western assumptions also underlie the thinking of Americans who associate happiness and personal well-being with consumerism and continuing technological progress. This emerging era of seeming convenience in accessing the data for controlling every aspect of daily life, from being able to turn on appliances while still at work to adjusting the watering of plants, to sending a steady stream of data about personal physical changes to the local medical provider, will be accompanied by the loss of privacy. The further loss of privacy will open the door to being subjected to an even greater barrage of advertising as the computer scientists and the cowboy capitalists promote the Internet of Everything as the new benchmark of modern development. Their innovative efforts and profits will expand exponentially as the Internet of Everything, including the hundreds of wearable digital devices marketed for children, is globalized.

The writings of leading computer scientists further reinforce this myth of linear progress. The myth is also supported by the steady stream of new digital technologies, as well as the reliance upon print. Both represent data, information, computer models, and videos as the basis of the highest form of intelligence.

Marginalized by the digital revolution are the forms of face-to-face, tacit, experienced-based, and intergenerational knowledge rooted in local cultural contexts and ethnic practices.

In effect, what cannot be digitized or fully represented in print are the face-to-face, relational, emergent, and semiotically rich cultural ecologies that are widely referred to as "cultural contexts." Daily participation in these cultural contexts requires constant decision making, negotiating meanings and deciding strategies of action, and an ability to situate these actions within a larger conceptual/moral framework. This is the level at which face-to-face and place-based democracy occurs. This is the deep democracy of a vital localism that can also be understood as the cultural commons. It is also the basis of the form of democracy that avoids hiding its colonizing cultural and economic agenda behind the abstract slogans of freedom, individualism, progress, and modernization.

The book's critique of how the hubris of computer scientists, cowboy capitalists, educators, and the number of people now addicted to reliance upon digital technologies, are undermining face-to-face democracy and the world's cultural commons is based on the insights of scholars who focused on how the dominant conceptual traditions in the West privileged abstract systems of representation over oral traditions of cultural storage, thinking, and communication. Central to their insights is the role of language in constituting the "reality" that people take for granted. Their insights, in turn, lead to recognizing the historical influences on patterns of thinking—including the mistaken idea that people are autonomous thinkers and that information and data are free of cultural influences. The ideas that help clarify how the digital revolution perpetuates many of the misconceptions of earlier thinkers in the West can be traced to the insights of Gregory Bateson, Walter Ong, Eric Havelock, Karl Polanyi, Clifford Geertz, and from what I have learned from indigenous cultures about the differences between individual and ecological intelligence.

Bateson's thinking provides the basis for moving beyond the conceptual frameworks of Western philosophers whose context-free rational (and ethnocentric) theories represented humans as existing independently of natural systems. Bateson's ideas also lead to recognizing that all life forming and sustaining processes need to be understood as cultural and natural ecologies, and to foregrounding the relational and co-dependent nature of the emerging relationships. The early chapters will examine the reasons many of the misconceptions inherited from the past, and that are part of the thinking of computer scientists as well as the public that have found their technologies useful (indeed, now essential) in carrying out so many tasks, continue to be taken for granted. These chapters, in effect, are meant to provide an understanding of the interplay between what the cultural languaging processes highlight, as well as what they marginalize in terms of awareness, and why so few people (including the computer scientists) are aware of the traditions that are being overturned by the digital revolution.

It is important to recognize that my focus on the deep conceptual reasons for challenging the idea that access to information and data is essential to a democratic society should not be interpreted as rejecting the importance of digital technologies. Like the technology of print, I am dependent upon using the Internet even as I am aware of its limitations. I am also aware of the dangers to democracy when narrowly educated experts overlook the cultural traditions being lost in a technologically driven approach to progress.

In the middle chapters I raise more focused concerns about the claims of computer futurist thinkers who extrapolate from Darwin's theory of natural selection that super computers will be displacing humans as the process of evolution grinds forward and who also argue that the primary purpose of the digital revolution is to change the world's cultures. Their hubris leads to a total lack of concern about the rights of other cultures to decide if they are willing to sacrifice on the altar of Western modernization the intergenerational knowledge and skills that are the basis of their own cultural commons. Like the narrowly educated computer scientists and their army of users and true believers, the assumption that the digital revolution must be globalized is based on a basic misconception handed down by the Enlightenment thinkers who were unable to distinguish between the oppressive traditions and superstitions of the feudal era and the traditions of the diverse cultural commons that were the basis of craft skills, artistic expression, food production and sharing, and mutual support systems.

A more complex and balanced understanding of cultural traditions is needed if we are to consider how the non-materialistic orientation of many of the world's wisdom traditions will be impacted by the digital revolution. Many of these wisdom traditions promoted the pursuit of lifestyles not centered on the consumerism and individual autonomy that contribute to deepening the ecological crisis. The question that needs to be asked is whether both the cultural commons that enable people to live less environmentally destructive lives as well as the wisdom traditions (which are also part of the cultural commons) will survive how the digital technologies are altering the consciousness of youth in ways that lead to viewing the knowledge of older generations as backward and no longer relevant. The chapter by Yusef Progler and Azra Kianinejad will raise similar questions about whether the leaders of Muslim cultures recognize the Westernizing influence of digital technologies.

The last chapter challenges the assumptions held by the computer futurist writers, as well as the wide range of public supporters who embrace every new digital innovation even as machines are able to increasingly mimic the explicit and procedural patterns of thinking that characterize many jobs, and even as the ever widening surveillance of everyday behaviors is transformed into data over which people have no control. The primary focus of the chapter is to highlight how the localism movement that is gaining momentum around the world represents an alternative to the increasing levels of unemployment, and the ways in which the digital revolution further enriches and increases the political power of the few at the expense the many. This movement, which can also be understood as the revitalization of the world's diversity of cultural commons that enable people to live less consumer and thus less environmentally destructive lives, restores a number of traditions such as the face-to-face accountability and intergenerational communication that are gradually disappearing as cyberspace increasingly becomes the medium in which communication and learning occurs. Face-to-face and place-based communities also represent alternatives to the electronically mediated relationships that are the sources of data being constantly watched by the emerging police state mentality of governments and by corporations seeking to take advantage of the consumer mentality created by years of advertising. The chapter also addresses what few people are willing to consider: namely, how people can prepare themselves in the event the worst case environmental projections become a reality; such as the growing acidification of the world's oceans, climate changes leading to devastating droughts, the loss of water, and the destruction of habitats. Local approaches to agriculture, control of essential resources such as seeds, soils, water, and forests—and reliance upon local currencies, systems of mutual support, and traditions of self-sufficiency in the arts and craftsmanship—are not romantic projections in the way that the computer futurists project the transition to a global management system by super computers that is dictated by Darwin's law of natural selection.

I must ask readers of my previous books to forgive the way I return to certain themes, especially those related to the formative power of the languaging processes that are not widely understood, and to the importance of the world's diversity of cultural commons. The recognition that most readers will not have read my earlier books accounts for introducing again the conceptual frameworks necessary for examining the cultural patterns reenacted in everyday life and thus to shifting the focus away from the world of abstract thinking. In addition to being indebted to a long list of scholars who challenged the orthodoxies of the last centuries, I want to thank Jennifer Knerr for suggesting the need to broaden the focus of the critique beyond that of the computer futurist writers, and Greg Smith for identifying changes that needed to be made in the first two chapters. Again, I need to thank my wife, Mary Katharine Bowers, for undertaking the onerous task of reading the first draft of the manuscript. Her suggestions, as before, have greatly improved the readability of a manuscript that can be challenging because of the introduction of concepts that may be new to some readers.

RECENT BOOKS BY CHET BOWERS

In the Grip of the Past: Educational Reforms that Address What Should be
     Changed and What Should Be Conserved
The False Promises of the Digital Revolution
An Ecological and Cultural Critique of the Common Core Curriculum

1

COMPUTER GLOBALIZATION

The digital revolution represents the West's latest effort to colonize the world's cultures. Unfortunately, its success is gaining momentum at the same time that a variety of forces, such as the expanding world population, the degradation of life supporting ecosystems, and climate change, are increasingly making life more stressful for the majority of people now moving toward the nine billion mark. A variety of motives have justified past efforts to colonize other cultures: the desire to control their resources, to create new markets, to rescue them from backwardness and superstitions, to strengthen the military of the colonized nation, and so forth. The current efforts on the part of computer scientists to impose their exceedingly powerful yet limited form of knowledge on the world's cultures is not unique in human history.

The titles of recent books by computer scientists are evidence of their hubris. Gregory Stock's *Metaman: The Merging of Humans and Machines into a Global Superorganism* (1993), Ray Kurzweil's *The Singularity is Near: When Humans Transcend Biology* (2005), and Eric Schmidt and Jared Cohen's *The New Digital Age: Reshaping the Future of People, Nations and Business* (2013) are just a few of the books by computer scientists who assume they have a special, even missionary, responsibility to save the rest of the world from the condition of data deficiency that impedes their ability to progress economically and technologically. As the title of the book by Peter Diamandis and Steven Kotler suggests, computers will bring *Abundance: The Future is Better than You Think* (2012) to the entire world. It is important to note that Diamandis and Kotler devote only a few paragraphs to the loss of jobs to computer-driven automation, which appears as an afterthought in the Appendix.

These computer futurist writers, as well as other Social Darwinian scientists such as Richard Dawkins and E. O. Wilson, envision a radically different future for humankind. Yet they do not discuss the many forms of resistance to Western colonization now dominating the daily headlines. In order for other cultures to accept the digital transformation they must undergo, as dictated by the computer scientists' interpretation of the Darwinian master narrative leading to the post-biological world of super-intelligent computers (also known as the coming era of Singularity), data must replace the authority of all other cultural forms of knowledge—as well as the wisdom traditions that are the basis of their moral values.

The above titles fit the definition of hubris, which is characterized by excessive self-confidence, an over-estimation of one's own competence, and the need to elevate oneself (or group) above others. Hubris can also be understood as part of the pathology that drives imperialistic and colonizing social movements. As will be shown in the following chapters, while computer scientists exercise a high degree of certainty about how the digital revolution will improve the lives of the world's diverse cultures, their mutually reinforced hubris has led to them ignoring the importance of learning about the belief systems and ecologically sustainable practices of different cultures. To make this point more directly: their fields of study, whether in the theoretical or applied computer sciences, require both a depth of knowledge and an ability to keep at the cutting edge of new insights and technological advances. This results in the double bind situation where their depth of knowledge in a very narrow field leads to new digital technologies being introduced without an understanding of the unintended consequences for the cultures into which they are being introduced. It is important to note that while the majority of computer scientists, venture capitalists, programmers, educators, and tech-minded people working to find more ways in which digital technologies can be used in everyday life are not likely to have read the futurist-predications of Gregory Stock and Ray Kurzweil, or the less extremist computer scientists such as Eric Schmidt and Peter Diamandis, they nevertheless represent a powerful social and economic force that threatens the intergenerational foundations of the world's various approaches to democracy and the equally diverse cultural commons.

Misconceptions that Limit Criticism of the Digital Revolution

Unfortunately, the narrow and highly specialized education of computer scientists that leaves them indifferent to the cultural traditions overturned by their tech-nologies goes largely unnoticed by the general public. This is due to the cultural lag perpetuated in universities, and thus in public schools, that has left most graduates with the same silences shared by the programmers, educators, venture capitalists, and the wide range of others engaged in spreading the digital revolu-tion into every facet of daily life—all in the name of progress. The reasons for the cultural lag, which can be understood as perpetuating the high status thinking in vogue during the last decades of the twentieth century, is easily understood. As most of a person's cultural knowledge, including that of professors, is taken for granted it is passed along to students at the same taken for granted level. Even the silences that accompany the interpretative frameworks that undergo minor elaborations as the professors' field of inquiry undergoes changes are passed on to students.

Unfortunately, the loss of the varied forms of knowledge, including wisdom, resulting from the increased reliance upon digital storage and communication in such areas as civil liberties, personal security from hackers, and the loss of intergenerational knowledge of how to live less consumer and environmentally destructive lives, goes largely unnoticed. The many conveniences, increased efficiencies, and forms of control that come from living in a connected world are taken to be more important than the traditions that are being lost. But then, traditions have always been represented in the corporate controlled media, in public schools and universities, as what must be overturned if a higher level of material progress is to be achieved. The high-status metaphors that supported viewing traditions as sources of backwardness include "change," "innovation," "new ideas and values," "experimentation," "progress," "critical thinking," "transformative learning," and "emancipation." That millions of Americans have not experienced progress in achieving a higher standard of living seems not to have diminished the power of the myth that change, especially technological innovation, will bring about a better future.

The important issue, however, is how the cultural lag perpetuated by the media, universities, and now digital technologies leaves students with the high-status knowledge of the twentieth century, which has been largely responsible for the problems we face in the twenty-first century. As the narrow and highly specialized education of computer scientists leaves them with little more than highly abstracted accounts of key ideas of Western philosophers, such as John Locke's explanation of the nature and origin of private property, Adam Smith's notions about the invisible hand and the progressive nature of competition and free markets (which Ayn Rand has turned into the equivalent of Moses' Mount Sinai moral tablets for governing all relationships), their simplified and reductionist ways of thinking lead them to assume that data, information, and other forms of abstract representations should be the basis of decision making for everyone in the world.

Before discussing why the cultural alternatives to the emergent digital culture must now become part of a critically informed public debate, it is necessary to take a conceptual detour that addresses what has been missing in the education of the majority of Americans who so willingly embrace each new digital technology, and who are unable to ask what is being lost that might contribute to an ecologically sustainable future. The following represents what students should have learned about the patterns that connect within their own cultural and natural ecologies—as well as those of other cultures. This missing background knowledge accounts for the widespread lack of resistance to the loss of traditions in the areas of work, civil liberties, creative arts, and patterns of mutual support.

Gregory Bateson put the problem somewhat differently. "The computer is only an arc of a larger circuit which also includes a man and an environment from which information is received and upon which efferent messages from the computer have effect. This total system," he continues, "or ensemble, may be said to show mental characteristics" (1972, 317). If the formal and informal educational processes in the last decades of the twentieth century had addressed the cultural patterns taken for granted by the innovators and supporters of the digital revolution, as well as by a public that is unable to question the digital narrowing of cultural knowledge and possibilities, perhaps the public would then have a more balanced understanding of the appropriate and inappropriate uses of digital technologies.

What is Common to all Cultural and Natural Ecologies

As the ecological crises are the dominant issues of this century, given global warming, the acidification of the world's oceans, the loss of species and habitats, and the multiple industrial chemicals that act like poisons surging through all plant and animal systems, it's time we adopt the world "ecology" as a way of understanding all life-forming, -sustaining (and -destroying) systems as emergent, relational, and interdependent. Understanding that there are no autonomous things, individuals, facts, data, events, ideas, and so forth, but that everything exists in a larger web of emerging relationships that have a history and possibly a future provided we acquire a more accurate way of thinking than what has been taught in public schools and universities. In the past, the word "context" was often used to refer to what was thought missing in references to an idea, a fact, an event, a behavior, and so forth. But this word, which signaled something more that needed to be considered, is also an abstraction, just as the world "culture" is an abstraction.

Referring to a conversation, the displacement of workers by robots, playing a game of chess, the violinist's participation in a group, a marriage undergoing stresses, and the purchase of the latest and biggest carbon-producing SUV, are all examples of ecologies. That is, the ecology of past ways of thinking (including the ecology of language that influences current thinking), ongoing and emergent expectations—including awareness of what is being communicated through the multiple information-rich cultural and natural pathways—characterizes every aspect of daily life. To make the point directly: there is nothing in the emergent nature of life that is static or independent of internal and external influences. The English language, especially the privileged status given to the use of nouns, as well as the reliance upon print and the abstract rational process of thinking that has been the legacy of mainstream Western philosophers, have marginalized awareness of the emergent nature of reality (or ecologies) that has been more easily understood in oral cultures.

Why emphasize the importance of thinking in terms of cultural and natural ecologies of emergent, relational, and interdependent? Why is this relevant as the digital revolution transforms every aspect of life into the wireless and increasingly connected world of data, facts, and information? There are a number of reasons that include the police state implications of governments acquiring data on people's behaviors, relationships, and communications without considering the cultural ecologies (contexts) of emergent relationships from which the data is collected. There are social justice reasons that go beyond the data on the number of workers displaced (the new "disappeared" from the middle class) by computer-systems, and there are ecological sustainability issues connected with the loss of intergenerational knowledge and skills as the Internet generation turns its back on the elders of their communities. But the most important reason for keeping in the foreground of thinking that all life processes need to be understood as cultural and natural ecologies is that the digital revolution is promoting on a global scale that the only forms of knowledge that should become the basis of decisions are abstract data, information, and models of the current and future behaviors of natural and cultural systems.

Plato and other Western philosophers helped to put the West on a Titanic collision course with the world's natural ecologies by privileging abstract theory over the forms of ecological intelligence developed to a high degree within many oral cultures. Driven by the myth of unending progress, computer scientists, and the army of their supporters and true believers (including uncritical consumers), are contributing to the globalization of data-based thinking and values. While data and information, on the surface, appear to be value free, both are interpreted by their collectors and promoters within value-laden conceptual frameworks that emphasize efficiencies, predictive control, continued innovation, and profits. In short, the moral framework supported by the emphasis on data is the market liberal ideology: that is, corporate capitalism that now aligns so closely with the abstract ideology of libertarianism.

Equally serious is how both print and data represent a world of fixed entities, of a moment of time in the emergent and relational world of a worker and of a consumer, and of other emergent and relational ecologies such as sending an email or making a phone contact with someone in a foreign country. What gets encoded in print or as data is only the surface phenomenon that the surveillance system is designed to represent as data. The immediate context, or emergent, relational, and co-dependent nature of the cultural ecology of a work situation or the behavior of a consumer, is not considered. The data and text that represents the information used to make judgments about a worker's efficiency, likely future consumer choices, and so forth, is at best only surface information. Yet it is used to predict future behaviors. But it is often enough for people, given the way the general public has been indoctrinated to accept what appears in print and represented as data and information, to adapt their behavior to fit the personal profile that is put together by the data brokers who are in the business of selling these data and thus abstract profiles to governments and businesses.

Print has had many important, indeed, indispensable, uses. Less noticed is that its dominant role in public and university education has led many people to take for granted the same process of abstract thinking that characterizes the limitations of print. The limitations of print can be easily recognized by standing in front of a crashing ocean wave, and then reading how the printed account of the event is unable to represent the full range of the emergent, relational process of a giant wave crashing against the rocks that also involves a wide range of senses, emotions, and memories of the observer as she/he backs away from the surging water. Print has enabled people to learn about the distant past and to reflect on what the future might be like, and it has enabled people to encounter the insights and ability of others to use the printed word in ways that bring clarity and the beauty of the insights of others—which often lead to insights into the fog of one's own taken for granted world.

But it has other characteristics that misrepresent the emergent and relational nature of cultural and natural ecologies that are the basis of life-sustaining processes—and of social life. That is, what appears in print represents a fixed reality open to being interpreted by the reader whose own process of thinking is often influenced by taken for granted cultural assumptions. It is also an immediately dated representation. Most importantly, the emergent and relational nature of experiences within the cultural and natural ecologies that cannot be fully represented in print and by data lead to abstract thinking where both are taken to represent reality. For example, the ways in which print leads to making the abstract more real than the emergent and relational nature of daily experience can be seen in how Western philosophers created abstract theories about the nature of knowledge, the source of values, the forces governing economic behavior, and so forth, without taking into account the cultural patterns enacted within their own communities—or the communities of other cultural groups.

Only the spoken word comes closer to representing the complex information (messages or what is communicated semiotically) circulating through the behaviors and patterns that connect within the interacting cultural ecologies. Speaking, listening, remembering, awareness of the full range of sensory experience, reflecting, and bodily movements are all part of interacting with the Others (both human and other-than-human) in the interdependent cultural and natural ecologies. What is often overlooked is that the spoken words of people socialized to think that the higher knowledge is acquired from printed texts too often take for granted that the following abstractions are real: "progress," "individualism," "freedom," "democracy," "literacy," "modernization," "free-markets," and so forth. Giving attention to how these abstractions influence behaviors in the emergent and relational world of everyday experience becomes irrelevant for literate and progressive thinkers socialized to view themselves as autonomous rational thinkers. That is, an over-reliance upon print-based cultural storage leads to patterns of thinking and communication that marginalize awareness of what is being communicated through the information pathways that are part of all relationships. The use of the above nouns, like other English nouns, does not lead to an awareness of relationships and the cultural patterns that connect. While the above abstract ideas supposedly have a universal meaning, when relationships change meanings, in turn, undergo corresponding changes. For example, the individual's experience in a consumer relationship or working at a repetitive task changes when engaged in a conversation of personal interest or in voluntarily helping others.

Ecological intelligence, as will be explained more fully when discussing how the digital revolution undermines the world's diversity of cultural commons, is exercised by everyone when they adjust their behaviors and thinking in ways that take account of the emerging and relational nature of passing another car, engaging in a conversation that rises above that of a monolog, in knowing when to enter into an ongoing musical performance, in adapting one's behavior to the timing required by an automated work process, and so forth. The exercise of ecological intelligence, in short, involves awareness of the emergent and relational patterns that are part of the ecology of information (semiotic) exchanges within which we live. Ecological intelligence is limited when relying upon abstract ideas, such as when the abstract idea of free markets prevents recognizing the connections between releasing billions of tons of carbon dioxide into the atmosphere and the rising rate at which the oceans are becoming acidic and thus are dying.

Ecological intelligence is also exercised by the person who is aware of relationships that involve prejudices and patterns of exploitation. This level of ecological intelligence is centered less on personal concerns about getting ahead, exercising control over others, and solving personal problems. In effect, it represents a social justice level of ecological intelligence where moral issues become a major concern. There is also a third level of ecological intelligence where the focus is on the relationships between personal practices, values, and consumer choices and their impacts on the sustainability of natural systems. Making consumer choices on what has a smaller carbon and toxic footprint, on pursuing a cultural commons lifestyle that reduces the need for consumerism and participating in the industrial/growth oriented economy, on reducing one's need for accumulating material goods, and so forth, are common examples of exercising an ecologically sustainable form of ecological intelligence. As will be pointed out later, many indigenous cultures, that is, oral cultures that did not encode their knowledge in books, developed complex forms of ecological intelligence by encoding the ecological wisdom about relationships in their vocabularies, ceremonies, and daily practices passed forward through mentoring relationships and face-to-face interactions.

The important question is whether the data and print-based information accessed on Google and other servers accurately represent the culturally diverse emergent, relational, and interactive systems within the cultural and natural ecologies. Or do the data and print (even video) representations reproduce the Western pattern of elevating what is fixed (that is, a world of things, events, and autonomous entities supposedly free of cultural and natural contexts) and seemingly objective reality over the emergent and interdependent world of ecological systems? That is, does the Internet transform what is emergent and exists as multi-dimensional semiotic exchange systems, ranging from the molecular to the global and reproduce René Descartes' seventeenth-century misconceptions of rational individuals living in an unintelligent and static material world?

Both the data and what is represented in print require being interpreted, which brings into play the taken for granted cultural assumptions that are too often the source of an ecology of misconceptions inherited from the past. For example, if the interpreter of data on the poverty among a certain cultural group is a follower of Ayn Rand's libertarian (objectivism) ideology, then the policies the data is used to support will be very different from the policies of the person who is a member of the impoverished cultural group. Unfortunately, the print- and data-based mindset fails to recognize the loss of cultural contexts, and that everything has a history. Later, the failure of the promoters of the digital revolution to understand the nature of cultural traditions will be examined more closely, as this failure is critical to understanding how the digital revolution bypasses the democratic process and why the reduction of the different forms of knowledge to that of information and data further empowers the elites promoting the digital/corporate culture.

2

THE CULT OF DATA

A Warning on the Misuse of Language

As I will explain in later chapters, the metaphorical nature of words, such as the word "myth," take on different meanings depending upon the cultural context within which they are used. In this chapter I will be using the word "myth" as it is widely used today in the West. The Merriam-Webster Dictionary provides definitions that represent the two different ways of understanding the nature of myth: first, as "an idea or story that is believed by many people but that is not true" and second, as "a story that was told in an ancient culture to explain a practice, belief, or natural occurrence." If we go to Wikipedia, which is increasingly replacing dictionaries that seem so yesterday, we find a more complex explanation—one that reflects the thinking of anthropologists who have studied myths. According to the Wikipedia entry on mythologies (which suggests how they influence thinking and daily practices), we find the following:

> The term mythology can refer either to a collection of myths (a mythos, e.g., Inca mythology) or to the study of myths (e.g., comparative mythology).

A mythology, as a conceptual/moral narrative or metaphorically constructed cosmology, is an important feature of many if not all cultures. According to Alan Dundes, a myth is a sacred narrative explaining how the world and humankind assumed their present form, although, in a very broad sense, the word can refer to any traditional story. Bruce Lincoln defines myth as "ideology in narrative form." He further suggests that myths may arise as either truthful depictions or over-elaborated accounts of historical events, as an allegory or personification of natural phenomena, or as an explanation of ritual. They are used to convey religious or idealized experience, to establish behavioral models, and to teach. As the Australian writer, James Cowan pointed out in a recent correspondence, if myth is understood only in the popular sense of being a story or ideology that is untrue, then today's descendents from the ancient cultures living in non-Westernized regions of the world, would be faced with acknowledging that their current lives are based on lies, misconceptions, and illusions.

In taking seriously Cowan's cautionary insights, I will be using the popular understanding of myth as an ideology or, in a more limited sense, as an idea that justifies a series of behaviors and values that are based on misconceptions and illusions essentially destructive to the well-being of community and the environment. I am staying with the popular usage, in spite of its limitations, as it suggests two conceptual patterns missing if I simply use "misconceptions" as the alternative to myth. That is, the popular usage still conveys the idea of ignorance, a misconception, or a deliberate lie that serves a group's special interests. The popular understanding also exercises the mesmeric power that limits the ability of the people to question the misconception. This leads in turn to double bind thinking where the acceptance of the myth (misconceptions and lies) leads to both short- and long-term destructive consequences.

One of the ironies is that the computer futurist writers, as well as many computer scientists and their collaborators within the digital industry who are working to reshape the world's future, would be the last to acknowledge that their deepest taken for granted assumptions are based on centuries-old Western misconceptions or myths. Nor would they be willing to admit that they are promoting new myths that are endangering a world fast moving toward a population of close to nine billion people. What the myths underlying their colonizing effort do not take into account is that this is also a world where billions of tons of greenhouse gases are being released into the atmosphere. The impact of these greenhouse gases is, in turn, accelerating the warming of the world's oceans, turning them more acidic (with the prediction that the pH level will reach 7.8 by 2100), and melting the glaciers that are the source of water hundreds of millions of people are dependent upon. These changes, in turn, are altering habitats and the life chances of species that have their own right to exist.

These life altering changes, which a few decades ago were predicted by scientists that appeared in newspapers and scholarly journals, are now impacting people's lives in the form of droughts leading to the higher cost of food, extreme weather that is destroying entire communities, and altered growing seasons. Climate scientists are now predicting that over the next 40 or so years nearly 50 percent of the world's population will lack adequate sources of water. The data for this prediction, unlike the data collected by data brokers and the National Security Agency on the behavior of people's everyday lives, is the kind that should be taken seriously. It should be leading to questions about how the cultural practices that have a smaller carbon and toxic footprint are being undermined by the digital revolution. The reasons for this silence will be considered when I discuss the increasing reliance upon computer-mediated education being promoted by computer scientists and programmers whose thinking is still mired in the assumptions of past centuries.

Given these challenges, plus the increasing dangers of cyber attacks on the nation's infrastructure and growing threats to our civil liberties, it would appear that the world has enough problems without suggesting that computer scientists and their collaborators are complicit in perpetuating many of the old cultural assumptions that underlie today's mythic thinking about unending progress, or what constitutes the Big Lie about the Big Data upon which most people seem happy to base their daily lives. Indeed, there are few challenges to the ways in which the myth of progress is used to justify each new digital technology.

The Myth of Progress Encoded in Moore's Law

Central to the myths being perpetuated by computer scientists is the idea of progress that Gordon E. Moore (co-founder of Intel) provided the metrics for measuring. In the paper he delivered in 1965 he predicted that the number of transistors on integrated circuits would double every two or so years. As this prediction has proved accurate over the last 50 years, it is now known as Moore's Law.

Moore's Law, which the semiconductor industry now relies upon to predict the rate of future technological developments and markets, has now become the code phrase for progress. First, it is not a law in the same sense as the law of gravity or the law governing the speed of light. Rather, the accuracy of his prediction leads to a formulaic way of thinking within the semiconductor industry that, in turn, is supported by one of the dominant myths in the West.

Since the early eighteenth century, advances in the development of technology, a greater reliance upon the scientific method, and critical reflections that led from viewing the individual as a subject in the stratified society of the feudal era to having the potential to participate in the political process, became the bedrock for thinking of progress as basic to how everyday reality is to be understood. This myth, which fits both Alan Dundes' definition of myth as a sacred (that is, an unquestioned) story and Bruce Lincoln's understanding of myth as a guiding ideology, is supportive of the way in which computer scientists interpret Moore's Law as yet another example of progress.

Moore's so called "Law" reproduces the longer held Western way of understanding progress as a technology-based linear march into the future. Unfortunately, this conceptual framework has troubling implications—especially when we take into account the rate of climate change and its local impacts. If we take account of what the myth of progress leads people, including computer scientists and a gullible public, to ignore, it is possible to recognize that the belief in the progressive nature of every new and supposedly improved digital technology will further divert attention from the many ways in which humankind's collective future is being put further at risk. Progress in creating computers that can be woven into clothes, worn as accessories like glasses and on the wrist, implanted under the skin, and so forth, will help the fashion industry to flourish, and to keep the chip manufactures busy. But this form of progress will further limit people's interest in recognizing and thus addressing how the industrial/consumer approach to progress is accelerating the rate at which natural systems are being degraded. The combined sense of amazement and the desire to acquire the latest technological gadget in order to communicate to others the cutting edge nature of one's lifestyle seldom lead to deep questioning.

Will wearable computers, for example, provide data on the amount of toxins that the computer industry is returning to the environment in countries where outmoded iPhones, computers, and other digital technologies are being recycled? Will these increasingly personalized computer devices enable their fashion-oriented consumers to be more aware of the amount of toxic chemicals being produced and used in the manufacturing of goods displayed and sold in ways that create the illusion (myth) of plenitude?

The myth of progress that frames and thus limits the awareness of today's computer scientists and their supporting public needs to be reconciled with the life-altering chemicals now being found, for example, in the umbilical cords of newborns. Blood samples of 10 newborns examined from different regions of the country were found to contain between 154 and 231 chemicals that included mercury, chemicals used in stain repellents such as Teflon, in flame retardants, cosmetics and plastics (Shabecoff and Shabecoff, 2008, 17). In some regions of the country one out of every 48 newborn males is found to have autism. Even the ability to collect data on the massive number of physical deformities and life threatening illnesses is a two-edge sword, as this data will be used by various groups to advance their own economic interests.

It is important to note that the scientists and corporate heads of the chemical industry also share the same view of progress that requires ignoring the adverse impacts on other life-forming and -sustaining process within both the cultural and natural ecologies. Computers are essential to this industry just as they are essential to the researchers at Monsanto and other companies engaged in producing genetically modified seeds that change the traditional relationships between farmers and the seeds, which they must now purchase each year. The progress of the Monsanto scientists that leads in turn to an ecology of economic dependence upon the corporations also includes dealing with the super-size herbicide resistant weeds that spring up 10 or so years after the regime of GMO seeds and herbicides are introduced. The myth of progress is also undermined by the ways industrially processed foods and the soft drink industry are adversely affecting people's health by exploiting their vulnerabilities toward ingesting excessive amounts of sugar and salt.

Perhaps the greatest challenges to the myth of progress are the many ways in which the Earth's natural resources are being exploited, contaminated, and degraded to the point where the prospects of future generations are being put at risk. Computer scientists have created the digital technologies that are absolutely essential to environmental scientists who are documenting the nature and rate of change in the viability of natural systems. At the same time, the alliance of computer scientists and corporations is creating the digital technologies essential to the globalization of the Western consumer-dependent lifestyle that is accelerating the degradation of environmental systems—including the billions of tons of carbon dioxide that are changing the Earth's chemistry.

That the computer industry is on the cutting edge of progress also needs to be reconciled with the loss of privacy and thus the loss of many traditional values. A more accurate way of putting the contributions of computer scientists in perspective is to ask whether the world their technologies are creating is safer for individuals who do not want their identities stolen, who do not want their values and behaviors shared with governments creating political profiles—or with corporations that use personal data to craft their advertisements and adjust their prices to fit the customer's preferences and economic status. There is also the question of how to reconcile the idea of progress, expressed so succinctly in the title of Peter Diamandis and Steven Kotler's book, *Abundance: The Future is Better than You Think* (2012), with the ability of hackers to penetrate the computer systems of governmental agencies as well as computer systems controlling the country's economic and energy infrastructures, and to making the theft of people's online accounts a new growth industry.

As computer scientists and corporations promote the global use of the digital technologies, the same threats will arise in other countries where the protection of civil liberties is less valued. As Julia Angwin points out in *Dragnet Nation: A Quest for Privacy, Security and Freedom in a World of Relentless Surveillance* (2014), the existential question that changes the quality of life for everyone is: Who is watching? And for what purpose? Another change that the digital revolution has brought about is the shift in power relationships in democratic societies. Access to power and money has shifted to those who own the data collecting and processing technologies. The ideas and values of the individual have become little more than collections of abstracted data that then become interpreted through the ideological lenses of those who use them to achieve their own political and economic ends.

Weighing the genuine forms of progress against the losses in individual privacy, in the ability to think beyond what can be tested by computers, in the viability of the democratic process, in the economic exploitation by those who own the data collecting technologies, and in the increased danger of cyber attacks, should lead to reframing how we understand what constitutes genuine progress. The political and economic uncertainties that accompany the spread of the digital culture also fail to slow the frenzied efforts to expand the level of consumerism, which is a major contributor to the millions of tons of green house gases and to the toxic chemicals that are threatening all forms of life. In light of these changes perhaps we should drop the word progress as a way of labeling this era of human development.

Connections Between the Myth of Progress and Ideology

Bruce Lincoln's observation that ideologies possess many of the same characteristics of modern myths helps to recognize the destructive impacts of the digital revolution. Modern history in the West has witnessed the influence of a number of ideologies. For example, market liberalism, which is based on a number of assumptions that underlie today's understanding of progress, has its roots in the thinking of John Locke, Adam Smith, Herbert Spencer, Friedrich Hayek, and Milton Friedman. Its underlying cultural assumptions have become reified over time to the point where they are now treated as universal truths. Marxism and fascism are also modernizing ideologies, with the latter having its roots in Social Darwinism thinking that is undergoing a revival as scientists such as E. O Wilson and Richard Dawkins step beyond the legitimate boundaries of the scientific method. Computer scientists such as Hans Moravec, Gregory Stock, and Ray Kurzweil combined the myth of progress and Social Darwinism into an ideology now used to justify the near total surveillance of people's associations, behaviors, and ideas.

A more recent progress-oriented ideology, which is gaining adherents across the United States, is libertarianism. Its conceptual foundations can be traced back to Hayek's *Road to Serfdom* (1944) and Ayn Rand's *The Virtue of Selfishness* (1964)—which she referred to as the philosophy of Objectivism. The latter has become for many Americans the sacred text of libertarianism. Ideologies, like modern myths, are based on a combination of narratives, abstract ideas derived from theorists who cobbled together a number of ideas of Western philosophers' abstract understanding of how reality is to be understood. Ideologies control thinking by providing the vocabulary that aligns everyday behaviors and values with the ideological conceptual map (or myth). The vocabulary is especially important in that it ensures conformity of thinking while at the same time excluding alternative vocabularies and thus alternative ways of thinking and acting. Excluded from awareness are the cultures based on different mythopoetic narratives and lifestyles—particularly those that pass their traditions forward as part of their cultural commons. Also excluded from the various progressive ideologies are the human wreckage and suffering caused by the practices of the winner-take-all mentality as well as the environmental damage hidden by the vocabularies of progress.

Libertarianism, which has now merged with the thinking and policies of the faux conservatives (who are actually market liberals in the Adam Smith, Herbert Spencer, Milton Friedman tradition of thinking), is based on a number of assumptions shared by many computer futurist thinkers such as Peter Diamandis, Eric Schmidt, Ray Kurzweil, Erik Brynjolfsson, and Andrew McAfee.

The principal ideas derived from Ayn Rand's writings include the following:

1. That the individual must always use rationality to attain his self-interest. That which threatens the individual's rational pursuit of self-interest is evil. Thus, the individual is totally responsible for his own success or failure.
2. In addition to leading a life of selfishness (that is, to pursue one's self-interest), the individual should be understood as a "trader." As she put it, "The trader is a man who earns what he gets and does not give or take from the undeserved. He does not treat men as masters or as slaves, but as independent equals. He does not switch to others the burden of his failures, and he does not mortgage his life into bondage to the failure of others" (1961, 33).
3. The only role of government is to protect man's rights: that is, to protect him from physical violence, to protect his right to his own life, to his own liberty, to his own property, and to the pursuit of his own happiness. Governments, in effect, have no right to penalize the strong in order to reward or help the weak.
4. If free market capitalism is to be free of governmental regulation, the values of altruism that distort understanding of the responsibilities of government must be replaced by the values of competition among men who rely upon their rational capacity to seek their own interests and happiness.

Other important assumptions that underlie Rand's ideology include the idea that rationality is culturally the same, that the "invisible hand" that operates in free markets ensures the continuation of progress, that technological innovations and market forces improve the quality of life for everybody, that there are no problems that cannot be solved by individuals pursuing their self-interest (Rand and her followers continue to ignore the ecological crisis), and that the cardinal principals listed above should be treated as universals that apply to all cultures. Given this view, if everybody lives by these abstract guiding principles and if market systems are under the control of the "invisible hand" rather than governments bent on redistributing wealth to those who have not earned it, there would be no social injustice—just the steady march of progress.

It is important to recognize that a significant percentage of the American population now take her ideas for granted even though they may not have read her writings. Equally important is how the libertarian ideology underlies the globalization of the digital revolution—including the silences in libertarian thinking and values. Rand, of course, did not possess the ability of Stock, Moravec, and Kurzweil, among others, to read the tea leaves that reveal the coming age of Singularity in which super computers will replace all organic processes, including human life. Nevertheless, the ideas that Rand claims will lead to progress and happiness are closely aligned with the thinking of computer futurist writers, and with the computer scientists focused on solving the technical problems of how to create more powerful and more widely used computers.

The following are examples of where the thinking of computer scientists and libertarianism come together.

1.   The autonomous individual is understood as the basic social unit within the sub-culture of computer scientists and their cultural colonizing agents. That is, for computer scientists such as Kurzweil who wrote *How to Create a Mind: The Secret of Human Thought Revealed* (2012), there is only one form of intelligence, and not a Muslim, Quechua, Orthodox Jewish or fundamentalist Christian intelligence. The possibility that there are other forms of cultural intelligence that have been influenced by linguistic differences and long histories of living in different bioregions introduces a level of complexity not encountered in the education of most computer scientists. Like the libertarian's indifference to the complexity of the world's cultural ecologies, there is no need to consider how the globalization of digitized knowledge and procedures could possibly represent the age-old process of Western colonization.

2.   Free markets, competition, and technological innovations are inherently progressive forces, which means one does not have to consider which traditions—including civil liberties, patterns of mutual support derived from the narratives of different religions and cosmologies, and traditions of exercising ecological intelligence—are being lost as individuals lead more data-based lives. Both libertarians and the culture of computer scientists are silent about what needs to be conserved as profit-oriented market forces, and the drive to reduce all life processes to data, further impede awareness of the social chaos beginning to spread as natural systems undergo even more extreme changes.

3.   Governments should not limit the ability of computers and market forces to do what they are designed to do: that is, provide all segments of society with the data that enables them to pursue their own economic, political, and social goals—which corresponds to Rand's idea that the selfish interests of the individual and corporation should guide the rational process. For the computer scientists, the exercise of rationality is furthered by access to more data. The focus on data as the source of rational empowerment does not take account of the taken for granted assumptions of the culture, or the assumptions of other cultures. Within the West, the deeply held assumptions (or root metaphors) that underlie the interpretative frameworks that are tacitly held include the idea of progress, the autonomous nature of the individual, a human-centered world, the mechanistic nature of all aspects of reality, economism (that is, everything has a price), and evolution. These cultural assumptions are also part of the taken for granted mindset of libertarians and market liberals (a.k.a. the faux conservatives).

As the deep cultural assumptions taken for granted by computer scientists are also shared by most academics, and by a public unable to escape the consciousness-shaping forces of the classroom, media, and the built culture, there are few people who are able to do more than complain about the loss of privacy, jobs, the traditional forms of personal security, and the increasing centralization of power in corporations and governments—including the local police who are becoming increasingly militarized. The challenge is to determine where to begin addressing how to live more community-centered (that is, face-to-face) and thus less consumer- and data-dependent lives.

People engaged in supporting lifestyles that are informed by what can be called ecological intelligence, which tends to be expressed in different local cultural and natural ecological systems—in political decision making, in the growing of food, in sharing skills and developing talents that contribute to the self-sufficiency of communities—are the most likely to take seriously the following discussion of what was and continues to be missing in the education of computer scientists that contributes to their extreme state of hubris.

Others who have become highly dependent upon computers, but are slowly awakening to the profound changes the digital revolution has introduced into daily life, may also be open to considering what was unthinkable just a few years ago. Namely, that the multiple advantages associated with computers may now be on the cusp of being out-weighed by what is being lost. My seemingly eternal optimism leads me to hope that some computer scientists will adopt the reflective stance taken by Bill Joy, the co-founder of Sun Microsystems who began to question the danger of technologies. Given how digital technologies are accelerating the rate of cultural change, computer scientists need to engage their colleagues in a discussion that goes beyond Joy's warning in his "Why the Future Doesn't Need Us" article (*Wired*, April, 2000). The discussion needs to focus on what we need to conserve in this era of deepening ecological crisis and growing police state surveillance. Hopefully, the following analysis may serve as guidelines for introducing the educational reforms that will enable computer scientists to ask: How do we innovate while also ensuring that important traditions are not lost in the pursuit of profits, personal achievement and reputations, and the hubris driven by what was not included in our education?

What Needs to be Understood About the Nature of Traditions

Essential to local decision making are the traditions intergenerationally renewed that serve as the legacy of the culture's past. They include the sources of empowerment, patterns of mutual support, as well as the prejudices that undermined the well-being of others. In short, without a knowledge of one's cultural traditions democratic decision making is too easily transformed by demagogs. Yet the chief promoters of technological progress such as Cisco, Google, IBM, Intel, Qualcom, and the millions of technological devotees, that are creating the wireless systems and Apps that will connect everything to everything, while reinforcing the traditions that underlie the industrial/consumer-dependent culture, perpetuate what Edward Shils referred to as the anti-tradition traditions in the West (1981, 278). How people's lives are influenced by cultural traditions is totally ignored by the computer futurist writers as well as the promoters of cloud computing such as Viktor Mayer-Schonberger and Kenneth Cukier. In *Big Data: A Revolution that will Transform How We Live, Work, and Think*, they claim the predictive power of big data "will fundamentally transform the way we make sense of the world" (2013, 72). "Transform" is their metaphor that is to be interpreted as progress.

The dominance of the idea of endless progress, especially technologically driven progress, has its roots in the thinking of seventeenth-century philosophers and scientists such as René Descartes, Thomas Hobbes, Isaac Newton, and Johannes Kepler. They held that reason is the only infallible guide and that the universe is a machine that can be scientifically understood and perfected. They also associated traditions with superstitions and the abuses of the feudal era. By associating traditions with specific beliefs and practices, particularly those of the church and feudal culture, rather than with the complexity of intergenerational knowledge of the local cultural commons that sustained the everyday life of the people who possessed the craft knowledge and skills used to build the magnificent cathedrals, the feudal era analogs chosen by Enlightenment philosophers for understanding the nature of traditions became the basis of thinking for the later educated classes committed to promoting economic and technological progress. Cultural traditions are studied in universities but they are represented as the achievements and limitations of the past. They are generally not represented as integral to today's cultural ecologies

For example, advances in the sciences, technologies, and in ameliorating the social injustice traditions of the past, were accompanied by changes in how the individual was understood—from that of a subject in the feudal era, to that of a citizen with the right to vote, to that of a creative being, and now to that of a self-made person who constructs her/his own world by accessing data and deciding where to go in cyberspace.

Formal education as well as the Internet provide access to knowledge of past and current traditions, but they do not provide an understanding of essential characteristics of traditions, including how they are the basis of so many aspects of today's taken for granted beliefs and daily practices—including the belief that as autonomous individuals we can rely upon technology and market forces to ensure that progress will continue.

These generalizations may appear as too sweeping, but the issues I am bringing into the foreground can be assessed by examining the writings of computer futurist writers such as Ray Kurzweil, Eric Schmidt, and Peter Diamandis, the justifications of computer scientists and the proponents of making computers available to every child in the world such as Nicholas Negroponte. Silence about the formative influence of traditions can also be seen in the ideological justification of Big Data, the technological entrepreneurs in search of the next App that will transform them into millionaires, the proponents of teaching young students to code, and the power brokers behind the common core curriculum such as Bill Gates and Rex Tillerson (CEO, ExxonMobil Corp.).

Where in their writings, and in their justifications for extending the digital revolution into more areas of daily life, do they mention the danger of losing traditions that are important to people's lives—and to the sustainability of the world's cultures and natural ecosystems? The irony is that while traditions are carried forward and modified in every sector of the dominant culture as well as in other cultures—from the network of laws stretching back to the Magna Charta of 1215 and beyond, in businesses small and global in reach, in education, medicine, and agriculture (including industrial/corporate approaches), and in the computer sciences and the other sciences—the influence of traditions remains largely hidden from explicit awareness. Their continued taken for granted status leads to ignoring what is being lost as new innovations in thinking, technologies, forms of economic dependence, and so forth are introduced. Just as there are no autonomous ideas, entities, and individuals, there is no absolute separation between the present and the influence of traditions.

Gregory Stocks' explanation of how the digital revolution is leading to the merging of humans and machines into a global super organism, which will also lead to the disappearance of the world's diversity of cultures, does not ask about the importance of the traditions that will be lost. Nor do Moravec, Kurzweil or the other computer scientists who think the world is entering the era of singularity dictated by Nature's evolutionary logic, even mention the fate of traditions that will be decided by the non-democratic process of natural selection. Even such acclaimed environmental scientists as E. O. Wilson exhibit an astonishingly naïve understanding of the power of scientists to be the ultimate arbitrator of which traditions are to be carried forward. As he put it, following his suggestion that all the religions of the world should be replaced by Darwin's metanarrative that explains the fundamentals of life, "science for its part will test relentlessly every assumption about the human condition and in time uncover the bedrock of the moral and religious sentiments" (1998, 265). Overlooked by his elevation of scientists to the Promethean role is their earlier support of eugenics and intelligence testing, and now the Social Darwinism claim that "memes" are the cultural counterpart to genes. The latter opens the door for ideologs to mask their political and economic agendas in the current language of scientism, which few people have the background to challenge.

These anti-tradition traditions of thinking are not limited to the various scientists, innovators, and supporters of the digital revolution. Because most of a culture's traditions are taken for granted, including the tradition of thinking that change, innovations, new ideas, expanding markets, and individual self-creation are expressions of progress that have the same power over peoples' lives as the law of gravity, few people are aware of the nature and importance of traditions. This is not to suggest that this lack of awareness means they do not reenact traditions, or that they are not aware of traditions after they have been lost. As will be discussed later when the focus turns to how the digital revolution is undermining the world's diversity of cultural commons, there are increasing numbers of people who are dropping out of the culture of unending progress, and who are responding to the deepening ecological crisis by consciously renewing more community-centered traditions that represent alternatives to the traditions of the industrial/consumer-dependent lifestyle.

Given the rate and range of cultural changes promoted by the digital revolution, the limitations of what is learned about the nature and importance of traditions in public schools and universities take on special significance. Indeed, when traditions are only recognized as sources of oppression, or only as a memory after they have disappeared, such as the memories of a pre-surveillance existence, they cease to play an important role in democratic decision making. In short, awareness of the nature and importance of traditions needs to be part of the democratic process of deciding what needs to be conserved, modified, and radically changed. When framed within a progressive/market-driven ideology that ignores the possibility that some traditions represent genuine achievements in how to live in mutually supportive and ecologically sustainable ways, democratic decision making is reduced to making choices between consumer-driven lifestyles—or to voting for the politician who uses the language of social justice but is not aware of the cultural roots of the ecological crisis.

So what should public schools and universities help students understand about one of the most important characteristics of their own culture, as well as that of other cultures now coming under the colonizing influence of the digital revolution? What do they need to understand as the digital revolution transforms nearly every aspect of daily life—from education, entertainment, health care, work, leisure, food production and preparation, to social networking where togetherness in the abstract world of cyberspace leads to more personal loneliness, as Sherry Turkle observed (2012). What do they need to understand about traditions, their own as well as those of other cultures, if they are to recognize how the myth of unending progress is being given new life by cloud computing?

Traditions: Another Way of Saying Everything has a History

The University of Chicago sociologist, Edward Shils, provides perhaps the most thorough and important understanding of what is most critical about the nature of traditions. He also addresses key misunderstandings about traditions that continue to affect daily politics—and now wars that are taking on a global reach. His overarching insight is that everything has a history and is part of an ecology of traditions nested in the interplay of cultural and natural ecologies. As pointed out earlier, the past continues to influence the present, and the present will in turn influence the future. Understanding the importance of this characteristic of all ecological systems requires doing what Clifford Geertz referred to as engaging in a "thick description" of the cultural patterns that are otherwise taken for granted (1973). A thick description of cultural patterns present to the senses, memory of past patterns—including past moral mistakes, dangers of hubris, and examples of the ways ecological intelligence have been exercised, should lead to an explicit awareness of cultural traditions. The question to be asked about the merits or wisdom of these traditions should be whether they contribute to carrying forward the genuine contributions of the past, such as the tradition of habeas corpus, the presumption of innocence until judged guilty in a trial by a jury of peers, local democratic decision making, a reflective and responsible use of print and data, and so forth.

A key point made by Shils about traditions is that what one generation may decide as representing a genuine contribution, such as Adam Smith's idea of free markets, and the "invisible hand" that guides all economic activity, may be understood by following generations as based on fundamental misconceptions about how markets exist in actual communities and may differ from culture to culture. Too often the taken for granted status of many of the ideas and cultural patterns handed down from the past are not understood as ecologically destructive traditions. They may not be understood as destructive within other cultures that were originally based on fundamentally different assumptions but have now come under the influence of the West's seductive metaphors of "progress" and "modernity." This can now be seen in how millions of people in China and India, as well as in other countries, are bent on following the Western model of a consumer-dependent lifestyle even as their health is being impacted by environmental pollution. The hundreds of millions of people becoming dependent upon consumerism, as well as the scale of technological/industrial and market forces, now overwhelm the possibility of self-correcting ecological systems.

That is, the double bind we now face is the way in which the conceptual assumptions that, taken together, underlie the god-word of "progress," continue to overturn traditions of mutual support and self-sufficiency. These traditions represent examples of community-centered democracy that often oppose governmental efforts to modernize people's lives by bringing them into a Western-style market economy. The particularly daunting challenge we face is drawing attention to both the language issues as well as how we continue to be in the grip of the past without a clear and agreed understanding of how to recognize and carry forward the genuine achievement of the past while rejecting what is now destructive. If we were to put to a vote the environmentally and community destructive traditions promoted by the digital revolution and its supporting market system, they would win by a wide margin.

Recognizing which traditions should be intergenerationally renewed is made even more challenging when we recognize another characteristic of traditions that Shils identifies. To reiterate an important point he makes: before anything, such as a new idea, practice, fad, technique, and so on, becomes a taken for granted tradition, it has to be carried forward over four cohorts or generations. This is the time interval that leads people to forget the debates and other features of the cultural/political context that gave rise to the innovation. What does not survive this four generation test, such as changes in slang and fashions, does not become a tradition. And as the individual's world of taken for granted thinking is continually reinforced by essentially the same metaphorical language that gave rise to the tradition, it also becomes part of her/his self-identity. These identity-shaping traditions include how to prepare a meal for a special occasion, how to dress in ways that meet other's expectations, how to adjust the size of the new car in relationship to changes in the price of gasoline and the expectations of one's social class. One of the traditions in terms of the latter example is to place self-interest above the concerns of others about further degrading natural systems.

The ecology of earlier misconceptions and silences, the ways in which the metaphorically influenced language handed down from the past perpetuate the old ways of thinking, the hubris and sense of entitlement magnified by the cultural emphasis on being an autonomous individual, and the lack of conceptual frameworks that provide alternatives to the environmentally destructive traditions, become major obstacles to a public discussion of which traditions are environmentally and humanly destructive, and which should be intergenerationally renewed. The problem is compounded as the Internet generation becomes more addicted to a technology that undermines awareness that the past continues to influence the present.

Shils' other observations about the nature of traditions are equally important to understanding the history of one's own culture as well as that of other cultures. He suggests that instead of thinking of traditions as self-perpetuating, that is as historical forces that operate independent of humans, it needs to be recognized that traditions are always carried forward by people who often misunderstand that traditions are as organic as the cultures that gave rise to them. People who assume that traditions should be viewed as timeless and unchanging make the mistake of turning them into the ideology that he refers to as "traditionalism." The reality, as he points out, is that traditions are very much like a plant with roots (traditions) extending deep into the nurturing soil (the past), and with some roots dying while new roots are emerging. He goes on to point out that some traditions should not have been started in the first place, such as exploiting child labor and selling people into slavery (which is still tradition in some cultures), while other traditions change too slowly, such as racial and gender biases.

Perhaps his most important observation about the nature of traditions is the one that is most relevant to the rate and scope of cultural changes resulting from the shift to data-based thinking that further erodes what remains of moral constraints on the supposed predictive power of data analysis. In discussing how traditions change in response to external forces and to internal innovations, Shils urges that reforming and overturning traditions should be based on careful reflection, as once a traditions ceases to exist, it cannot be recovered. The loss of privacy to the web of surveillance technologies is perhaps the best example of how new digital technologies were introduced without regard for their unintended consequences. What other traditions are being threatened by the ideological and economically driven rush to rely increasingly on decisions based on the information and data acquired on the Internet? The list includes all the traditions in the areas of the food production and sharing ceremonies, creative arts and crafts, narratives, games, social justice gains that were passed forward through mentoring and face-to-face relationships. The list also includes the moral values and patterns of mutual support that are learned and reinforced in the face-to-face interactions within most non-Western cultures—as well as those still passed forward in Western cultures.

Just as spell-check makes it unnecessary for students to learn how to spell and the key-board makes it unnecessary for learning to write cursive, recipes and health remedies available on the Internet make it unnecessary to learn from the intergenerational knowledge learned and refined over many generations, and robots in the workplace make it unnecessary to remember when workers controlled the pace and methods of production—that is, before Frederick Winslow Taylor popularized the scientific management of work. Mentors in the crafts ranging from working with fibers, wood, and metal are also being displaced as the digital generation turns its attention to video games and creating a sense of community from the abstract images and words shared on social networks. Fortunately, many youth and adults find learning from the Internet and life in the social networks to be shallow and unfulfilling in terms of developing personal talents and participating in communities of shared interests.

The digital revolution does not represent the beginning of technologies that undermined and displaced traditional knowledge and abilities. As stated earlier, it is the source of important and often missing information. And its convenience cannot be overstated. But the basic issues with regard to its role as the latest in the anti-tradition traditions of Western science and market capitalism brings us back to the question of how both print and data represent only a surface account of the emergent, relational, and interactive nature of embodied human experience. Regardless of the activity, life-forming and -sustaining processes within the cultural and natural ecologies, whether in mentoring talents in a creative art such as jazz or learning to save seeds for next year's planting, what is learned is dependent upon passing forward traditions refined over generations. But this process of intergenerational renewal also requires learning to be critically reflective about whether the traditions reproduce the misconceptions and biases of earlier eras, that should not have been constituted in the first place—or should be conserved because they represent hard-won earlier social justice achievements.

These are not the concerns of the computer scientists who are developing robots for the military, replacing the need for workers with computer systems, and creating the Internet of things where everything will be constantly monitored and subject to external controls.

An example of the future can be seen in the request by the European Union that technologies be installed in cars that allow the police to turn off the engine, regardless of where the car is, if the driver is a suspect. Other "progressive" research includes developing the technologies that eliminate a person's bad memories, which could easily become a way for authorities to alter the memories of the person who challenges the environmentally destructive practices of the coal industry or the practices of other industries. Social justice and environmental issues are not the concerns of programmers who write the curricula for public schools, or the digital entrepreneurs creating apps for acquiring data on the number of steps a person takes in a day or the number of calories that can be reported to friends on a social network site. These digital revolutionaries may not go as far as Ray Kurzweil, Hans Moravec, and George Dyson in proclaiming that we are entering the post-biological era where super-intelligent computers will govern the world, but they share the same vision of a progressive future that makes irrelevant knowledge of the cultural changes they are introducing and the importance of the traditions being lost.

To return to an important point that is too often overlooked: if traditions that are the source of personal meaning, self-identity, and empowerment (and are not sources of exploitation and prejudice) are taken for granted, they can be overturned before there is an awareness of what is being lost in the name of progress and increased profits. Of course, people who do not understand the differences between traditionalism, where it is assumed that traditions should not change, and the organic nature of traditions, create a special problem that the abstract and fixed nature of print exacerbates.

An Old Anti-tradition Tradition on Steroids: The Incessant Quest for Profits

The global spread of the free market system is also based on a number of cultural assumptions and values that lead to equating the overturning of traditions with the anti-tradition tradition thinking and practices inherent in corporate capitalism. The primary value of the capitalist system is achieving the greatest possible level of profits. This leads to overturning many traditions such as the idea of an ideologically free Supreme Court, the independent judgments of the people's representatives, and the ability to learn in environments that represent a psycho-social moratorium free from the influences of corporate values that reduce all aspects of life what contributes to the bottom line. The impact of the West's market economy and technologies is an anti-tradition force in every country that seeks to become modern and economically developed. As in the case of the anti-tradition traditions that science and technologists are promoting in the name of progress, as well as the subverting influence of market values, there are few examples of ecologically and culturally informed discussions of the nature and importance of traditions. The elites being interviewed in the media, as well as the success in responding to the incessant drive to produce the new knowledge that determines the fate of academics, are yet two more examples of how we are still caught in the grip of the Enlightenment obsession with overturning traditions, even those that are vital to our ecological future and well-being as a civil society. The metaphor of progress is one of those context-free metaphors that makes critical and informed thinking appear as unnecessary, even as hackers continue to overcome the corporate and government security systems and police departments adapt their tactics to the total information systems that are now available and acquire the military weapons that send the message about who is really in control.

3

MISCONCEPTIONS ABOUT LANGUAGE

Silence about the reality constructing nature of language is not unique to the education of computer scientists and to most public school and university graduates. Nearly everyone in Western-dominated approaches to formal education encounters the same silence. Computer futurist writers, such as Ray Kurzweil, Eric Schmidt and Peter Diamandis, and computer scientists working on a wide range of digital solutions to human and environmental problems, as well as the promoters of extending the digital revolution into more areas of everyday life (including child reading and all levels of formal education), have not acquired an in-depth understanding of the "reality constructing" role of a culture's languaging processes. The following is meant as a primer that addresses this basic failure in public schools and universities. In the following overview, it is important to continually consider whether the varied promoters of the digital revolution are aware of how the language they take for granted may be perpetuating the misconceptions and silences of the past. Environmental scientists are warning that the growing world population, along with the spread of the consumer-dependent lifestyles that are overshooting the sustaining capacity of the Earth's natural systems, are reducing the margins of survival for future generations. And while these scientists do not address how the promoters of the digital revolution are unaware of how the languaging processes they take for granted reproduce ecologically destructive cultural assumptions, the warnings of the environmental scientists should serve as a wake-up call for everyone who is uncritically embracing the new myths of a digital future.

The widespread indifference to the role of language in influencing what people experience as "reality" is dependent upon a series of basic misconceptions in the West. The misconceptions include the following: (1) That the language used to communicate what is experienced as reality is fully accurate in its representations;

(2) That language operates as a sender/receiver system of communication, or what Michael Reddy refers to as a conduit through which ideas, data, and information are objectively conveyed to others; (3) That the spoken and written uses of language are the primary modes of communication—a view that excludes the semiotic patterns of communication within both cultural and natural ecologies; (4) That the reification of what is communicated, including the long-standing myth that language operates as a sender/receiver model of communication, leads to assuming that other people experience the same reality. Reification refers to losing sight of the cultural/human origins both of the language (vocabulary) and the people who represent their ideas and observations as a form of objective reporting.

These misconceptions are, in turn, supported by the assumption discussed earlier: namely that the printed word is the basis of objective knowledge even though it is unable to accurately represent the dynamic, emergent, and relational processes occurring as people interact with each other and with the environment. To reiterate two other key points: print also fosters abstract thinking and that words are metaphors that carry forward the misconceptions and silences encoded in the analogs settled upon earlier but now taken for granted. It also undermines awareness that all language systems are culturally influenced human creations.

The conduit view of language is being reproduced—along with the other characteristics of language mentioned above—as print, graphs, dynamic models, and streamed visual and oral performances appear on the computer screen. If the above misconceptions are not taken into account, what is learned from computer screens, and from the use of other digital devices, perpetuates the misconception of communication as being a conduit through which objective data, information, ideas, and so forth are passed.

The important point that relates most directly to why computer scientists, programmers, and educators who are relying more heavily upon computer-mediated learning should recognize these misconceptions is that whatever technology that appears on the screen—the printed word, the graph, model, and the streamed talk or event—has a history and thus carries forward earlier patterns of thinking that may not accurately represent today's world. This is the problem Gregory Bateson identified as the conceptual map (created in the past) that does not accurately represent today's territory (issues and relationships we are facing today). This will be discussed further when the complexity of metaphorical thinking/languaging processes is addressed.

A second problem that computer scientists, along with most other Americans victimized by these silences, do not recognize is how they contribute to undermining the moral narratives and deep cultural assumptions of other cultures—many of which have not made individualism and the pursuit of material wealth their primary values. In addition, many of these non-Western cultures have developed lifestyles that represent humans and natural systems as part of the same moral/ecological world, and thus do not reduce these natural systems to being exploitable resources. Everything, when understood in terms of their relational existence, participates in multiple patterns of communication within the larger cultural (in the case of humans) and the natural ecologies within which humans participate. Their identities are as complex and transformative as the information pathways that are part of the interdependent and emergent ecological systems within which they participate. Yet the English noun-dominated language is unable to represent their relational and emergent nature. In effect, it focuses on the dancer and not the ongoing dance—on the "think-about-which-is" rather than the "thing-which-is becoming" to quote Rupert Ross (2009). This difference has important implications for how people have been socialized to think of data as representing a fixed event, behavior, idea, and so forth. When the world, from the micro to the macro level, is understood as ecological systems, then it becomes easier to recognize what data does not take into account.

Basic Understandings About the Linguistic Roots of Cultural Ways of Knowing

One of the unfortunate characteristics of specialized disciplines is that new insights and even major paradigm shifts too often stay within the originating discipline. This results in scholars working in other disciplines not benefiting from the new insights. Another problem is that too often the scholars within the discipline that have gained the new understandings fail to explore their implications for introducing reforms that would slow the rate of environmental degradation. This is definitely the case with all the misconceptions identified above. I did not originate this list of misconceptions, but acquired an understanding of them from scholars working in the sociology of knowledge, ecological and cultural linguistics, and intellectual history. To support the point made about scholars not exploring the ecological implications of their new insights, none of the following—Peter Berger, Walter Ong, Mark Johnson, George Lakoff, and Don Idhe—mention the ecological crisis, and thus have ignored how their insights help to clarify the cultural roots of the ecological crisis.

Role of Language in the Cultural Construction of Reality

The subtitle of this section should read: "Be careful about imposing your vocabulary upon other cultures—including future generations within your own culture." When a culture's linguistic roots are overwhelmed by the vocabulary of another culture, which seems to be occurring as Asians adopt the vocabulary of the West's digital and industrial/consumer-oriented culture (partly because many of their intellectuals were educated in the West after World War II), the loss of their vocabulary means a loss of a complex ecology of historically refined knowledge of relationships, achievements, and even errors made in the past. What few agents of linguistic colonization recognize is that English nouns represent a world of distinct entities while other languages more accurately represent the emergent nature of relationships within the interdependent cultural and natural ecologies. They also ignore how most English words are metaphors whose meanings were framed by the analogs that encode the cultural assumptions and silences of earlier periods in the West.

In *The Social Construction of Reality* (1966) (especially Chapter 1) Peter Berger and Thomas Luckmann explain how language is essential to reproducing the view of reality taken for granted by previous generations. The key point they make is that people do not experience some aspect of the world and then use their "own" words for communicating about it to others. Rather, in being born into a language community, the process of socialization involves acquiring the vocabulary and the underlying assumptions necessary for thinking and communicating with others. The language handed down over generations, even with slight intergenerational modifications, provides the conceptual basis for understanding what is encountered through the senses, as well as the abstract representations of reality learned from others. Too often the reality-constituting language inherited from the past makes it difficult to be aware of patterns in experience that were not recognized in the past. For example, it should be obvious that the supposedly autonomous individual reproduces the conceptual patterns passed forward in the process of socialization, yet people continue to think of themselves as having their "own" ideas and making their "own" value judgments. This pattern of thinking exhibits another linguistic legacy: namely, that everything is understood differently depending upon which relationships and contexts are being considered. The idea of individual autonomy becomes recognizable as a misconception when the connections between language and thought are considered. Similarly, the idea of progress appears justified when considering advances in technologies and in civil liberties, but it appears as a myth when considering the various technological impacts on natural systems. Differences in relationships lead to differences in how the participants are understood. In effect, nothing exists entirely free of other influences except for when it is forgotten that abstract ideas and data have a human authorship. This is where print and digital technologies contribute to losing sight of human/cultural authorship.

An example of not recognizing that the words we associate with expressing our own ideas have a history, and as metaphors that carry forward the assumptions and silence of earlier eras, can be seen in how many people think of free markets and progress. The questions not being asked by the people who take these ideas for granted include: where did we get the idea of free markets since it is impossible to experience a market that does not take place in some physical/cultural context? Where did we get the idea that change leads to progress? Did the idea come from the abstract thinking of theorists who ignored the nature of cultural contexts? The idea of free markets can only be encountered in the printed texts of theorists. As an abstract idea it then becomes part of people's reified conceptual frameworks used to interpret the world, but never examined in terms of local contexts. The same process of not examining the abstract idea of progress in terms of its impacts on local cultural and natural ecologies could be easily carried out except for its taken for granted status. The list of print-derived abstractions not only includes the idea of free markets, but individualism, freedom, emancipation, science, technology, and so forth. Science, for example, should be understood as a verb, as it represents exercising a particular form of intelligence. To reiterate, print cannot fully take account of cultural relationships and the complexity of contexts, but leads easily to being misunderstood as representing a universal and objective reality.

Berger and Luckmann make several other points crucial to understanding the power of language. First, even though most of the vocabulary is handed down over many generations (again with modifications and updates in terms of what are considered more appropriate analogs) what is passed forward through socialization is seldom explained as having a distinct cultural history. That is, the meanings of words are initially experienced as providing an objective account, and not as the interpretation or misinterpretation of previous generations. Thus, human authorship and the culturally specific nature of thinking are ignored. Second, as words and interpretative frameworks simultaneously illuminate and hide, the process of learning the language of one's culture does not include, in most instances, sharing the important insight that language, operating as an interpretative framework, limits the possibility of alternative understandings. Third, the reality represented by the language to which one is being socialized by others often becomes experienced as taken for granted—which leads to what can be referred to as a natural attitude that marginalizes awareness of the need to raise questions. Thinking of the environment only as a natural resource, change as inherently a progressive force, and intelligence as an attribute of the autonomous individual, are examples of taken for granted beliefs—in the same way English speakers organize thoughts in terms of the pattern of subject, verb, and object.

Fourth, as people undergo the same process of primary socialization of how to think within the conceptual analogs encoded in the culture's vocabulary, most share with other members of the language community the same misconceptions and silences. This can be seen in the shared vocabulary within the computer science community where such words as "data" and "information" exclude other vocabularies such as "sacred" and "wisdom." If one reads the writings of computer futurists such as Moravec, Stock, and Kurzweil, the dominant vocabulary is derived from the root metaphors of progress, individualism, and a human-centered world. The words "conserve," "tradition," and "ecologies" do not appear, even though these words more accurately relate to most aspects of human experience.

What computer scientists do not understand is how different vocabularies encode different cultural ways of knowing and traditions of experience that have been refined over centuries. In the case of the West, data and information reproduce a cultural epistemology that privileges abstract, print-based thinking and storage as more valid than oral traditions that rely upon all the senses, memory as sources of information, and the information pathways connecting the emergent and relational world of cultural and natural ecologies. Meanings can be negotiated in oral cultures, which is not the case when the reader is learning something for the first time or encountering what is constantly repeated in a written text. Computer scientists, and misinformed educators, are constantly arguing that computer-mediated learning is a source of empowerment—which again is an abstraction that most people are willing to accept on face value. But what is the cultural context within which the individual exercises this empowerment?

Generally overlooked is that reading involves an asymmetrical power relationship made even more complicated by the lack of awareness of how one's own taken for granted conceptual framework has been influenced by the earlier forms of intelligence (or unintelligence) encoded in the metaphorical language acquired in the process of socialization. While there have been attempts to explain the metaphorical nature of language and thus of thinking as a process of encoding bodily experiences in the neural networks of the brain (Lakoff and Johnson, 1999), this approach misrepresents important characteristics of metaphorical thinking, including the role of metaphors in the linguistic colonization of other cultures where data and information are displacing other metaphorical vocabularies. Students who are encountering the curriculum on the screen of a computer, researchers relying upon the Internet, and computer futurists who are writing about reshaping the future of other cultures, are all relying upon the metaphorical language that is dominant in Western cultures.

That most words are metaphors and thus have a history is one of the silences that accompanies the myth that language functions as a conduit in a sender/receiver process of communication. If it were widely understood that earlier forms of intelligence, including misconceptions, prejudices, and silences, influenced the choice of analogs that frame the current meaning of many words, there would be more widespread questioning of the idea of objective information, data, and rational thought as being free of cultural influences. The current meanings of words such as "Indians," "tradition," "intelligence," "ecology," "progress," can be traced to earlier eras when the taken for granted cultural assumptions and evocative experiences influenced the choice of analogs that framed the meaning of these words. Referring to God's intentions in terms of "His Will" or actions (which not only anthropomorphizes but also assigns masculine qualities) is a clear indication of how earlier ways of thinking are reproduced in current vocabularies and thus ways of thinking.

The basic process of analogic thinking occurs when the new is understood "as like" an older pattern, such as how the passing of germs is explained to young students as like passing a football. Too often the analogs encode "as like" ways of thinking that carry forward basic misunderstandings that have a lasting influence. This can be seen in Columbus' mistake of thinking he had landed on the shores of India and that the dark skinned people were Indians, in the Enlightenment thinker's failure to recognize that the intergenerational knowledge and skills of the cultural commons are part of life-saving traditions, in the misconceptions of Western philosophers who gave us such abstractions as the "rational process," the "autonomous individuals," and "private property" as though they were free of taken for granted cultural assumptions. The analogs for understanding the Greek word "oikos" should have included many aspects of daily life, including local customs. Over time the analogs were simplified to the point where their meaning was reduced to the study of natural systems when it should have been understood that ecology applies equally well to the interactive and emergent languaging/behavioral patterns we call culture.

What are the implications for computer scientists, programmers, and classroom teachers whose hubris has made it unnecessary to question what is becoming increasingly obvious to anyone who is aware of how the feminists challenged old analogs and introduced new ones that more accurately represent their past and current achievements? Have all computer scientists ignored that creating a near total surveillance society that strengthens the control of corporations and governments, and has undermined many civil liberties, is inconsistent with the traditional meaning of the word progress? Moving from an imperfect democracy to an increasingly efficient police state can only be understood as progress by the wealthy oligarchy that benefits from this transition. Are computer scientists unaware that everything in both cultural and natural ecologies communicates, and that oral traditions are essential to carrying forward personal and communal memories that are more complex and important than the data and surface information they are attempting to elevate to the highest and most dominant form of knowledge?

One of the consequences of ignoring print and other abstract systems of representation that enable people to communicate is how they marginalize awareness of the information/semiotic exchanges that sustain life in the cultural and environmental ecologies within which they are situated. As mentioned earlier, words and interpretive frameworks (e.g., the earlier mentioned root metaphors such as mechanism, progress, etc.), like other aspects of a cultural ecology, have a history. When this is ignored, as in software programs used in schools and in the writings of computer futurist thinkers, there is a loss of cultural memory.

Words and other images then create the illusion of an autonomous present—in meaning, in factuality, in existence. Ignoring that everything has a history that influences the ecology of emergent relationships leads to not questioning what needs to be conserved. Should craft knowledge and skills be intergenerationally renewed? Should traditions of privacy be carried forward? Should people have a way of earning a living or is the quality of their lives less important than the efficiencies and profits gained from the computerization of the workplace? Should students be free to make mistakes without their youthful indiscretions becoming part of the data profiles being collected on them and stored in corporate and government data bases? What about the traditions of other cultures that should be carried forward and intergenerationally renewed? Which traditions contribute to an ecologically sustainable future and which should be reformed or abandoned entirely? These questions are absent in the writings of the computer futurist thinkers who view themselves as providing colleagues with the big picture of their incremental role in shaping the destiny of humans. Indeed, these questions are also missing in the growing number of books raising concerns about the digital transformation of cultures that have bypassed the democratic process. These deep cultural issues, including how the digital revolution reinforces ecologically destructive cultural patterns, are not mentioned in such recent books as Sherry Turkle's *Alone Together: Why We Expect More from Technology and Less from Each Other* (2012), Robert W. McChesney's *Digital Disconnect: How Capitalism is Turning the Internet Against Democracy* (2013), and Evgeny Morozov's *To Save Everything, Click Here* (2013).

There is a plausible explanation for why computer scientists and their army of tech supporters do not ask questions about what needs to be conserved as the ecological crisis deepens and as life is made more uncertain from the threats of cyber attacks on the nation's infrastructure. It has to do with the power of language to influence thinking and thus awareness. Moore's "Law" as well as the number of digital technologies that enable people to undertake tasks previously unimaginable provide a record of experience that supports the more widely held cultural myth of progress. The personal wealth, increased status, and economic growth of the computer industry, which far outstrips other sectors of the economy, also insulates highly intelligent and narrowly focused computer scientists from any doubts about what the future holds.

The chief ideologs of the computer sub-culture also strengthen the idea that there is only one way forward for the world. A sub-title of the last section of *Abundance: The Future is Better than You Think* (2012) by Peter Diamandis and Steven Kotler, puts it simply as "Unstoppable." This declaration of absolute certainty about the future of the human condition appears after a three-page discussion of "Robots, AI, and the Unemployment Line" that appears at the end of their book as an afterthought. Following a reference to Bill Joy's warning about the unintended consequences of computer technology, Diamandis and Kotler make a claim that is remarkable given the widely known evidence of environmental changes that can in no way be interpreted as signs of progress. They end the book with the following: "Considering the gravity of these concerns and the continued march of technology, reigning in our imagination seems the worst plan for survival … there will always be holdouts (again, the Amish), but the vast majority of us are here for the ride. And, as it should be clear by now, it's going to be quite a ride" (303–304). The reference to the Amish is Diamandis' and Kotler's way of suggesting that if we don't embrace their vision of the future, we too will be like the Amish whom they consider to be icons of backwardness—which again reflects their lack of understanding of the diversity of cultural lifestyles.

If Kurzweil's prediction is correct that the evolutionary transition to the era of Singularity will mark the end of human life, then the Diamandis and Kotler vision of progress will indeed be quite a ride. The takeover by super-intelligent computers that will plan their own future designs, and manage the global network of super computers, and even have religious experiences as Kurzweil claims, is a strange way of understanding progress. Indeed, it borders on being pathological. Yet the view of progress shared by computer scientists and their army of supporters, which encompasses many of the technologies now used to exploit others, need not be subjected to public discussion and democratic decisions.

If computer scientists and the general public, as well as computer futurist thinkers, who are really the ideologs of this increasingly dominant sub-culture, understood the complexity of the cultures they are transforming, questions about reducing opportunities to earn a living, about living in ways that are free of police state levels of surveillance, and about passing forward the knowledge and skills essential to living less environmentally destructive lives, should be central in their thinking about the cultural transforming nature of the technologies they develop. As mentioned earlier, their failure to ask these questions is partly due to the failure of public schools and universities to promote an understanding of the cultural transforming nature of different technologies. Cultural lag is real, and can be partly attributed to the hubris of university professors who think they are on the cutting edge of progress, but are actually reproducing with only minor variations the interpretative frameworks they learned from their mentors who were unaware of how the deep cultural assumptions they reinforced in their teaching and research were contributing to the ecological crisis.

This hubris is especially prominent in the thinking of professors of education who view their missionary role as ensuring that students march to the current drumbeat of progress, which now requires more reliance upon computer-mediated learning. The supposed progressive nature of this technology is that it allows students to construct their own knowledge—which is another myth that goes unquestioned by the computer/curriculum suppliers who want to sell more curriculum materials and computer testing systems.

4

DIGITAL COLONIZATION

A combination of reasons account for why computer scientists lack an understanding of the symbolic foundations and daily traditions of non-Western cultures as well as their own culture. That their own sub-culture has evolved into one of super-rich high achievers has further reduced the need to question the impacts of their technological and economic agenda on cultural traditions that nearly all thoughtful people would vote to keep. The lives of most computer scientists, as well as other people, are guided by a surface knowledge of the social rules and expectation of others. The result is that critical reflection about their own cultural assumptions is of little concern. To them, the language that sustains the conceptual and moral orthodoxies shared by others in their sub-culture also provides the safe haven necessary for taking on the real challenges, such as creating new computer programs that increase efficiencies in different work settings, modeling changes occurring in global weather patterns, and moving the frontier forward in the emerging fields of nanotechnology and bioengineering. Developing neural implants that improve memory and the systems for driverless cars are the real challenges. These are also the frontiers where the new markets will be—along with wearable technological systems.

Why should computer scientists waste their time thinking about whether their culture-changing technologies should be subject to the democratic process that includes people other than corporate decision makers who think first and foremost about the profitability of new technological breakthroughs? And why should they devote time to asking about how the digital revolution they are promoting on a global scale is undermining other cultures that have not entirely embraced the West's assumption that all traditions are sources of backwardness? The stereotypical thinking that guides the daily lives of computer scientists also serves as their taken for granted understanding of the needs and values of the rest of the world, even though they have little understanding of the diverse cultural and environmental forces that are reducing a huge percentage of the world's population to a life of impoverishment and hopelessness.

Progress in achieving a better material life is an unachievable abstraction for several billions of people. Their needs are more specific, such as the need for food, water, and security in order to sustain life for another day. For those who see a glimmer of hope that their circumstances can be improved, the digital revolution opens doors that previously seemed closed. Cell phones connect people over vast distances and the Internet provides information that increases access to markets that, in turn, lift people out of dire poverty. For parts of the world where the digital revolution is making its first impact, progress can be measured in economic numbers, including the numbers of cell phones, Kindle readers, people accessing the Internet, and revenues from online advertising directed at the emerging middle class in various countries.

For computer scientists and the corporations economically and ideologically intertwined in promoting the digital revolution, little else needs to be known about these non-Western cultures. Vast fortunes are being made without questioning the loss of cultural traditions that can be written off as the nostalgia of the older generation still conceptually unable to overcome the digital divide. It seems common sense to computer scientists to assume that the entire world wants the material and other benefits of progress—especially the digital forms of technological progress. As in the West, the rising use of digital technologies can be interpreted as a vote of the people that is a more accurate representation of their preferences than stuffing their votes in a ballot box. And the number is rising into the hundreds of millions of users.

The writings of computer futurist writers such as Stock, Moravec, Schmidt, Diamantis, and Kurzweil have also provided the conceptual and moral basis for ignoring such seemingly obvious ideas that the voices of the people of other cultures should be heard about which Western technologies they are willing to adopt. As pointed out earlier, Darwin's theory of evolution, which Stock, Moravec, Kurzweil, and Diamandis have turned into the ideology of Social Darwinism, provides a façade of scientific justification for ignoring the traditions of non-Western cultures that might lead to the charge of cultural colonization. Indeed, why bother about cultural traditions that Nature has programmed for extinction in order for the better adapted cultural memes of the computer scientists to take over? Rather than relying on the Social Darwinism of their colleagues, Eric Schmidt and Jared Cohen justify their vision of progress in the following way:

> If the destruction of institutions and systems caused by upheaval has a silver lining, it's that it clears the path for new ideas. Innovation exists everywhere, even in the labored and intricate work of reconstruction, and it will be

enhanced with a fast network, good leadership, and plentiful devices, meaning smart phones and tablets.

(2013, 239)

In being more specific about the "next 5 billion people to join the club," as they put it, Schmidt and Cohen add that they "will be net beneficiaries of the connectivity, experiencing greater efficiency and opportunities, and an improved quality of life" (ibid., 254). They might have added that in being technologically emancipated from the traditions that shaped their identities and communities, they might experience the further benefit of beginning to think like Americans.

The tensions between the West and the rest of the world go back centuries. They have become more intense, however, as technologies have increased the power to project Western ideas of modernization and development, as well as economic and military interests, around the world. These forces of colonization, often promoted by Western-educated leaders from within the colonized cultures, continue to meet resistance—which is increasingly taking the form of the armed struggles we are now witnessing in Muslim cultures. There have also been more peaceful forms of resistance such as the Chipko Movement in India, the continuing struggles of First Nation cultures across Canada, and the various indigenous resistance movements in Central and South America. Indeed, there are few regions of the world that are free of local resistance movements now being reinvigorated by an awareness that the deepening ecological crisis is yet another way in which the influence of the West is impacting their cultures.

The alliance of the computer industry, international corporations, and the military is now the dominant force promoting such core values of the West as individualism, consumerism, a democratic system of government that is dependent upon the West's idea of the autonomous individual, and what the late sociologist Edward Shils called the "anti-tradition traditions" of the West. The Internet, social media empires (both American and foreign), commercial media giants, and global corporations totally dependent upon digital technologies for every phase of their operations, are now a common feature in every country in the world—except for a few countries such as Bhutan that has developed its own approach to assessing what constitutes progress.

Instead of relying upon economic indicators for determining a country's gross national product, the Bhutanese measure Gross National Happiness by taking into account a complex set of wellness indicators that cover all aspects of cultural life, including the physical, mental, workplace, environmental, social, political, and economic activity. Unlike the non-Western countries that have adopted the West's economic metrics for determining the rate of progress, the Bhutanese, as they have in the past, consider how the adoption of a new technology will affect all of the nine indicators of cultural and environmental wellness. They have a more complex, indeed ecological, way of recognizing and thus resisting foreign colonization. In spite of this there are early signs that their youth are beginning to embrace Western consumer values.

Colonizing Other Cultures: A Misguided and Dangerous Effort

The history of Western approaches to colonizing other cultures ranges widely: from military invasions, religious conversions, economic domination, educating their leaders to think like their Western mentors, equating happiness with consumerism and media images, and educating their youth in Western-style schools. Colonization usually involves winners and losers, with the winners usually being the colonizers. There have been benefits to those being colonized, such as the spread of ideas about the rule of law, the nature of social justice, sharing of scientific knowledge and technologies. The benefits often appear over many generations after the initial shock, economic disruptions, and violence have subsided. But the memories of overturned traditions, economic exploitation, and a general sense of being subservient to the colonizing culture, also survive—and often become the basis of armed resistance.

What is noteworthy about the different forms of colonization in recent history is summed up in the title of William Easterly's book, *The Tyranny Experts* (2013). As he notes, the experts who have guided these different forms of colonization have not taken a bottom-up approach where they first learn from the local knowledge and traditions. Rather their approach is to assume that their own knowledge and technologies are superior, and thus to adopt a top-down strategy for imposing their ideas. As Easterly points out, "the West's approach to developing and modernizing non-Western cultures following the end of World War II was based on the assumption that the cultures needing development should be understood as a blank slate" (24–29). That is, these cultures were to be viewed as possessing little in the way of knowledge and cultural achievements that needed to be taken into account when forming a development strategy. The outcome of the top-down approach benefited those who understood development in economic terms, which meant Western corporations. What the experts wrote off as no more significant than a blank slate were the local cultural traditions that did not fit the ideology driving the developmental strategies. As development and modernization are primarily understood by experts as being economically measurable, recent forms of colonization have meant participation in a Western-style market economy—thus becoming a satellite of the Western economy.

The important issue widely overlooked in the current efforts to globalize the digital revolution so "the next five billion people can join the club," as Schmidt and Cohen put it, is that it is also a top-down approach that precludes the exercise of local democracy. In using the phrase "local democracy" I do not mean that people will not be allowed to mark a ballot about whether they wanted their youth introduced to cell phones, laptops, the Internet, and so forth. Rather, I mean that local voices, especially the voices that reflect an understanding of how these technologies would Westernize their youth, are not being heard.

Instead, the immediate conveniences, as well as politically and economically important uses of these technologies, led adults to adopt these technologies before there was an in-depth understanding of the local face-to-face and inter-generationally connected cultural commons that would be lost. The media campaigns that accompanied the promotion of digital technologies also exploited another ploy of the colonizers, which is to imply that adopting the technologies will bring people into a modern and connected world. And the metaphor of "modern," as it does in so many parts of the non-Western world, carries with it images of happiness, drudgery-free lives, endless consumerism—and always, seemingly rich smiling faces.

While the conveniences and economic benefits for those who need to reach markets outside of their immediate vicinity are undeniable, less publicized is that the daily dependence upon these seemingly magical technological gifts from the West will further increase their dependency upon a money economy. Becoming more dependent upon a money economy, while the digitally driven industrial system undermines people's traditions of meeting their daily needs by relying upon local crafts and production skills, involves yet another double bind. The industrial system of production and distribution reduces the need for the inter-generational skills that sustained local markets while at the same time creating a global market system where the work is increasingly done by computer-driven machines.

Becoming dependent upon digital technologies requires another fundamental shift even greater than that of leaving the oral traditions behind in order to adopt a print-based mode of cultural storage and thinking. As pointed out earlier, digital representations, storage, and thinking do not reproduce the complexity of daily life in the local cultural and environmental ecologies. It's not that all pre-dominantly oral cultures are free of the language issues, prejudices, and the silences of earlier generations that limited a critical awareness of how to resist the forces of colonization. Far from it. But many of these predominately oral cultures have acquired a knowledge of local ecosystems that is quite astonishing compared to what most literate Westerners understand about the ecosystems upon which they depend.

Survival for these oral cultures depended upon their ability to adapt their values and practices to what the natural systems could sustain. And in order to adapt daily practices it was necessary to be careful observers of the information circulating within and between the local ecological systems. Oral cultures also have a more complex understanding of the importance of the non-monetized cultural commons, which can be seen in many ethnic cultures where traditions of self-sufficiency are still carried forward. One has only to ask the most highly print-dependent and thus abstract thinkers about the nature and importance of their cultural commons and the response will be a blank stare as they head into the nearest mega-consumer emporium.

Why the "One Laptop per Child" Educational Reform Failed

Western missionaries understood that if the long-term transformation of a non-Western culture was to succeed it would be necessary to re-educate the children to the colonizer's way of thinking. As the colonization of indigenous cultures spread across what was to become the United States, one of the strategies was to punish children who spoke their mother tongue. A similar strategy underlies the current effort to rescue students from economic poverty by introducing them to a new pattern of thinking. In the current jargon, the challenge for the development experts is to overcome the "digital divide."

The leader of this effort to promote the digitally based cultural pattern of thinking among the children of the world is Nicholas Negroponte who is an MIT professor. Like the well-intentioned yet self-serving interests of other colonizers, Negroponte proposed a top-down expert driven approach to ending global poverty by providing every child with her/his own inexpensive and durable laptop. The idea gained wide support among hi-tech companies and philanthropists, which led to the creation of the non-profit Cambridge-based One Laptop per Child Association (hereafter OLPC) which Negroponte headed. Momentum quickly built behind this seemingly revolutionary approach to achieving higher educational outcomes that would eliminate poverty, accustom the youth of the world to using the Internet as their primary source of information, and to living in a connected world that overcomes the isolation of their communities and the supposed backwardness of their largely oral-dependent parents. By 2012, OLPC reported that over 2.5 million laptops had been purchased by or given to ministries of education in over 19 countries spread around the world.

This top-down approach to promoting literacy and economic development was based on a number of misconceptions held by the mostly Western-educated officials in the different ministries of education, by Negroponte and the support groups in the OLPC, and by the classroom teachers in countries ranging from Peru to Mongolia. The myth that technology is simply a tool and thus culturally neutral was held by all of these supporting groups. In addition, another powerful misconception rooted in the ideology of progressive education assumed that students learn best when they construct their own knowledge, and work collaboratively with other students. By providing access to vast amounts of information, data, and visual representations of cultural events, computers were seen as providing students a way of avoiding the limited and dated knowledge of their teachers. An equally important misconception that had been reinforced by the UNESCO decades-long program for eliminating illiteracy was the assumption that literacy provides access to the high-status forms of knowledge that underlie modern and scientifically based industrial societies.

The local cultural traditions that did not fit the development experts' understanding of the blank slate that was to be transformed by giving every student a laptop included the complex oral traditions, the cultural commons, and the wisdom traditions that, in many cases, were the basis of mutually supportive communities and the exercise of ecological intelligence. As understanding the complexity of oral cultures, as well as the ecologically destructive nature of the scientific/industrial/consumer-dependent cultures, was not a strength of these development experts, including Negroponte and his supporters, the outcome of their hugely expensive experiment in social engineering came as a surprise.

What happened in Peru was replicated in the other countries where the laptops were introduced. The reasons for the failure of the top-down technologically driven reforms become especially clear when we consider the case of Peru. More than 800,000 low-cost laptops were distributed to children across the country, at a cost of over 200 million US dollars. This top-down approach to educational reform did not take account of the need to educate teachers about the cultural transforming nature of computers, which might have led them to engage students in a discussion about the appropriate and inappropriate uses of digital technologies. Nor was there any effort to enable teachers, many of whom were from urban areas and thus inclined to view local knowledge as having lower status, to understand how to integrate computers into the curriculum that still contained nearly 30 percent local content.

These failures can be attributed to a widespread inability among computer scientists and program developers to understand the cultural transforming nature of computer-mediated learning. This shortcoming in the thinking of the experts, which is also replicated in the thinking of American teachers, was only part of the reason that this huge expense, as well as the expectation that technology would lead to fundamental social reforms, failed so completely.

I had been in Peru a few years earlier when the Western-educated Peruvians in the Ministry of Education initiated country-wide educational reforms that required more Western content in the sciences and mathematics, along with a de-emphasis on local knowledge. These reforms reflected a deep prejudice on the part of the urban-oriented Ministry of Education toward the supposed backwardness of the rural and largely agriculturally oriented population. Local knowledge that was the basis of one of the world's most bio-diverse approaches to agriculture was to be replaced by Western knowledge regarded as having a higher status. That this was largely irrelevant in the lives of the rural population did not matter. I also witnessed the introduction of the new reforms that promoted the students' construction of their own knowledge. This was an idea that led American educators to embrace computer-mediated learning as it was thought that students would have access to unlimited information. That students might lack the conceptual frameworks necessary for using the information to clarify important social and ecological issues was not a concern. Indeed, the American educators thought that if the teacher were to provide students with different explanatory frameworks for understanding how the world works, it would have been seen as an imposition on the students' ability to construct their own knowledge. Negroponte's global agenda for lifting the world's youth from the supposed backwardness of their oral cultures was simply a matter of following the formulaic thinking that was in vogue among American educators.

The outcome of the OLPC top-down experiment should have been predictable to anyone who understood the local cultures into which these laptops were introduced. But as the local cultures represented what experts understood as the blank slate (that is, the knowledge of the students' parents) from which the laptops were to rescue the students, the expectations of the experts were notable only in terms of how badly they misjudged the influence that the laptops actually had on the students' education. A study of the gains in 319 Peruvian rural schools found "no increase in math or language skills, no improvement in instruction quality, no boost in time spent on homework, no improvement in reading habits" (stuff.co.nz/technology/72117599). In the higher grades researchers found that students were using their laptops for playing online games and visiting Facebook.

The students were being introduced into the West's world of abstract thinking as the bits of information that represent only a snapshot of the behaviors and other interactive processes in the life-supporting ecologies appeared on the screen. The bits of information taken from an emergent, relational, and information-rich Quechua world was experienced by students as facts, objective information, and explanations that encode someone's interpretative framework—while the context from which the data was taken was ignored. Students accustomed from an early age to reading books and playing video games may not give thoughtful attention to the differences between the more complex sensory world of direct experience and face-to-face communication and the world of printed representations and the dynamic digitized images that are now so life-like. As the background of Peruvian students involved being immersed in the sensory world that requires memory of how the emergent and relational world works, as well as in the oral world of mentoring and ceremonies, it is not surprising that students were unmotivated by what appeared on the computer screen. For them, learning was part of face-to-face relationships in a world of physical changes, as well as taking responsibility for carrying out tasks that were shared and reinforced by others. The life-world of the students did not prepare them for the solitary experience of responding to the printed words and abstract images appearing on the screen.

There are too many cultural variables to accurately determine the effect of laptops on learning. If the culture has a long tradition of print-based cultural storage and thinking, such as many cultures in the West and in other parts of the world, then the transition to computer-mediated learning may meet less resistance than when the student is from a predominately oral culture. It is interesting to note that a study of several Ethiopian schools found that the laptops had improved abstract thinking. Was there a tradition of literacy, or other cultural traditions that may have influenced this outcome? Learning in predominately oral cultures is participatory and involves all the senses, embodied memory, and awareness of the shifting cultural patterns through which multiple forms of information are being communicated. Print, to recall earlier discussions, primarily involves sight, memory of other abstract representations where local contexts are ignored, and little that connects to the students' self-identity and need for meaning.

What is particularly interesting about Peru is that experts such as Negroponte, given that he shared the same lack of in-depth understanding of his own as well as other cultures (reflected in his proposal to parachute computers into several Ethiopian villages so children could learn to read), assumed that the software programs loaded on the laptops would provide a superior education than what the students could learn from their local culture. Students, in effect, would be encountering the culturally influenced mindset of the people who write the software, which would not be different from encountering the mindset of the people who write the textbooks—except for the interactive relationships missing in textbooks. In effect, the shared assumption is that the student is encountering a higher and better informed intelligence, and that the knowledge of the local cultural and natural ecologies is unimportant.

If Negroponte had bothered to study the culture of the Quechua and Aymara living in the regions extending from Peruvian Amazonia to the altipano by Lake Titicaca that borders Bolivia, he would have quickly learned that this ecologically diverse region has been designated by UNESCO as one of the 12 sites in the world with the greatest diversity of plants, including edable foods. For example, the diversity of potatoes found in the different ecological zones is estimated at 3000 varieties. In an Aymara village, 200 varieties of potatoes were found in a two-and-a-half acre plot.

The cultures of this region of the world cannot be written off by the blank slate metaphor that was taken for granted by the promoters of the OLPC global programs. If Negroponte and his colleagues had bothered to investigate the intergenerational knowledge not only of how agricultural practices are passed forward but also the ability to "read" the behavior of animals and birds as sources of information about changes in weather patterns that are so critical to knowing when and where to plant and when to expand or reduce the number of animals, they would have encountered the complexity of ceremonies, patterns whereby elder knowledge is passed forward, and a cosmology that represents humans and nature as existing in reciprocal nurturing relationships. As students participate in working in the fields, in the ceremonies, in learning the medicinal properties of plants that surround their dwellings, and in learning to recognize how they are being nurtured by Pachamama, sitting in front of a laptop could only be an isolating experience devoid of meaning.

The top-down approach of Western experts precluded learning about recent approaches to education in Central and South America that represent alternatives to how government schools alienate students from their local cultures. These indigenous oral cultures are developing approaches to education that avoid students being colonized by having to learn the abstract knowledge important to the careers of computer programmers and foreign professors but unrelated to learning the community skills necessary for sustaining life in their bioregion—and "to be in the minds of the community when something is to be done," as Jorge Ishizawa and Grimaldo Rengifo (co-directors of PRATEC) put it (2011, 175). This is profoundly different from meeting the minds of the computer scientists and software programmers who lack a sense of a morally connected universe, and who also lack an awareness of the importance of the ecological intelligence passed forward as mentors and learners engage in the regeneration of local knowledge and skills.

The non-technological approach to education being promoted in the rural areas of Central and South America is profoundly different from the Western expert's understanding of how computer-mediated learning is necessary if students are to connect to the empowering world of abstract data. Inspired by Mexico's Universidad de la Tierra or Earth University, which reflects the decolonizing educational insights of Gustavo Esteva and Guillermo Bonfil Batalla, Peru's UniVida has a threefold agenda that differs radically from the cultural colonizing process inherent to the print-based curriculum students encounter on the laptop computers. It is an approach that could be adopted in any culture where educational reform is focused on the intergenerational renewal of the local cultural commons, and on reducing the impact on the Earth's ecosystems. As Ishizawa and Rengifo explain the Schools for Living Diversity:

> In UniVida, school does not mean classrooms. The schools for living diversity are places for the regeneration of the modes of thought, action, and innovation of the Andean Amazonian peoples, and for acquainting students with other cultures. They are "spaces for intercultural confidence," or places for intercultural nurturance. Their objectives are:
>
> 1. To affirm community youth in their own cultural values by reflecting on their role in the nurturance of the Andean Amazonian territories and the cultures they shelter.
> 2. To provide the space for the understanding, from their position as young community members, of the challenges brought about by modernization of the Andean Amazonian region.
> 3. To create *in situ*, an experience of intercultural relations with young people from other cultures.
>
> *(ibid., 177)*

These guiding principles have led to the creation of the School of Biodiversity and Food Sufficiency, the School of Community Skills, and the School of Intercultural Dialogue. Learning in all three schools (which are not conventional classrooms) takes place in different settings where students interact with members of the community who have skills and ecological knowledge to share. Learning is face-to-face, and what is shared is how to exercise ecological intelligence—that is, to be aware and interpret the information and other semiotic signs of how to nurture relationships in both the local cultural and environmental ecologies.

A curriculum that emphasizes abstract data and information, as well as technologically mediated communication with others, may lead to acquiring computer skills and learning to read. But this approach, even when carried out at a level that approximates that of scholarly research, seems less important than learning how to live more community-centered and less environmentally destructive lives. Computer scientists are making important contributions to advancing the work of environmental scientists, but there is little evidence that anyone in their subculture understands how digital technologies are undermining the traditions within their own culture, or those of other cultures, that put less carbon dioxide, toxic chemicals, and that transform natural systems into the mountains of trash suffocating parts of the world's oceans and filling huge landfills.

This lack of knowledge of the interdependence of the local cultural and natural ecologies led to attributing the failure of the OLTC program to Peru's lack of technological infrastructure, low rate of literacy on the part of parents, and the poor training of teachers. These criticisms reflect a mentality that was unable to recognize the basic community and environmental values that the people, in spite of their limited participation in a money economy, were making a central part of their children's education. Quechua parents want their children to understand the modernizing changes taking place, but they also want them to be well grounded in the ecological intelligence basic to their food security in the biologically diverse and changing world.

I am not suggesting that we copy the traditions of the Amazonian Andean cultures, but their achievements, as well as those of other predominately oral cultures, should lead to asking if our over-reliance upon technologies, including the technology of print, may be one of the reasons for the near culture-wide silence about the cultural changes we must undertake if we are to survive the multiple impacts of climate change.

What the experts, including environmental scientists, are telling us is that we need to find new technologies that will mitigate the adverse environmental impacts. However, they are silent, as are most professors and nearly all classroom teachers, about the non-technological reforms that must be undertaken. They also mirror the computer scientists' lack of understanding of the largely non-monetized traditions that have not entirely been lost to the economic and technological forces driving the process of globalization.

5

THE DIGITAL REVOLUTION IN MUSLIM CULTURES

Joseph Progler and Azra Kianinejad

How the dominant cultural values of Western industrial consumerist society are carried over into the digital age may not be recognized if the culture undergoing colonization does not have a history of examining the cultural mediating characteristics of social and mechanical technologies. Furthermore, asking what cultural traditions are amplified and reduced by the introduction of different technologies is not likely to happen if the culture being colonized has already accepted the Western myth that technology, in itself, is neutral, and whether it is used for constructive or destructive purposes depends upon the agenda of the people using it. In order to obtain a clearer perspective on the degree to which the digital revolution is understood within a Muslim culture such as Iran as having a Westernizing influence, it is first necessary to summarize the cultural transforming characteristics of the digital technologies now being globalized. As we examine debates about what constitutes the appropriate use of the Internet for educational, social, and religious purposes, this summary will help bring into focus what is being identified as having a Westernizing influence, and what remains unrecognized.

The first characteristic of digital information technologies is that they reinforce and normalize several dominant cultural values of the West, including the assumption that represents high-status knowledge as abstract, context-free and depicted in print and now in data. Thus, it is detached from face-to-face community-based relationships. Communication technologies and social media, while promoting the illusion of connecting people with each other and with information, undermine face-to-face and intergenerational relationships with the past, with one another, with knowledge of the environment. These relationships are central to the place-based, community-oriented forms of knowledge that have nourished cultures for centuries. As computer users relate more with machines than with one another, they are prioritizing the conceptual and moral authority of abstract data detached from people and places.

These devices and data are not subjected to the ecological imperative of living within the limits of a locality, and become instead subservient to economic and political forces far beyond the locality. This is because the interpretation of information and data, when separated from face-to-face relationships where there is potentially an element of accountability, often involves a shift in power relationships where the interpreter's agenda can lead to reframing the meaning of the information and data. Furthermore, the digital technologies that users tend to see as universal neutral tools reinforce an individualized subjectivity that undermines past ways of knowing, including various forms of community-based wisdom.

While digital technologies may superficially appear to be more convenient, there is a trade off in that the forms of knowledge that are made lively and vibrant within ecologically aware place-based communities and face-to-face forms of communication are lost, forgotten, or deemed irrelevant. The abstract forms of knowledge made possible by digital technologies that are understood in the West as expressions of progress undermine the ecological modes of awareness that encourage people to take responsibility for their own social actions and for living by the moral imperatives of caring for one another and their shared environment, which has traditionally been based on a reciprocal understanding of the interdependencies of a relational world, including its cultural and natural ecologies.

When discussing the impact of digital technologies on culture it is vital to take into consideration the terms of the debate and the framework within which these issues are usually discussed. A common framework is to perceive information and communications technologies in terms of their promise and peril. Although it is not always or even usually acknowledged in debates and discussions about the impact of digitization, proponents of both views are often limited in their understanding of the cultural and ecological dimension. The focus is largely on the promise of digitization, the view most often promoted by the technology industries, which is frequently reproduced without question by academics and policy makers. When voices emerge pointing to the perils of adopting the West's digital technologies, they are limited to such issues as national sovereignty, cultural identity, and survival of the dominant political system. Or they are fixated on the threat of importing foreign media. To some extent, both viewpoints represent culture as a site of conflict and each side brings evidence to support its perspective, but the overall understanding of culture, whether in terms of promise or peril, is narrow and severely limited. What we aim to do in this chapter is to point out the third, neglected dimension of these debates and discussions.

At the center of the Iranian national debate and silences about the appropriate uses of digital technologies is how they are viewed as connecting people and information to one another, while they are actually bringing about a separation of people from one another and of knowledge from its cultural context. However, this is not a conspiracy or plot, as is often claimed by those on both sides of the debate; detachment is inherent in the use of digital technologies and in the way they are talked about. There are several Western-root metaphors promoted by the use of digital technologies that serve as taken-for-granted interpretive frameworks, such as individualism, hierarchy, progress, and control. Computer-based information processing exacerbates a subjective form of individualism, even narcissism, by reinforcing the feeling that people are autonomous and independent beings, and that what is needed is a network of digitized information to connect these autonomous individuals, and that learning and decision making are most efficient when they are based on increased access to digital information—thus allowing "individuals" to construct their own knowledge and determine their own values.

In terms of hierarchy, the role of computers and digitization in what is commonly referred to as the "digital divide" is often recognized, but this is limited to political and economic hierarchies. What is not acknowledged is the hierarchy that puts digital knowledge at the top and relegates non-digitized forms of knowledge to the bottom or margins in terms of importance. In this sense, the social, economic, and political hierarchies that often overlap questions of race, ethnicity, religion, and gender, which are all very real and necessary to rectify, are too often limited to making an appeal for more access to digitized information, which does not address the hierarchy and prejudices encoded in different forms of knowledge.

The metaphor of progress, which represents change as beneficial and headed toward some mutually advantageous but hazily defined goal, obscures these other forms of knowledge further by promoting the idea that science and technology will discover all the answers to human problems and needs. This reinforces the Western view in which traditions come to be seen as an obstacle to progress. The metaphor of control, proceeding from the view of human dominion over nature, is further narrowed to the question of management instead of the broader consideration of the implications of a belief that humans have a mandate to exploit and shape nature to their own selfish ends. The collapse of control into management further marginalizes those forms of knowledge that are still relevant and vibrant within the myriad vernacular traditions of the world. In the end, this severely undermines local participatory decision making and the intergenerational and face-to-face cultural commons that are less dependent upon a money economy.

When discussions of digitization and the impact of computers on society are dominated by questions of who has access and the mandate to promote their agendas, there is a loss of awareness of the deeper cultural and ecological issues that the entire world now faces. To reiterate a critically important point: when we understand how culture is being redefined as that which can be digitized, then we may recognize how the current debates within Iran are limited in scope because they do not go beyond reproducing the achievements and proclamations of the technological industries. If we fail to appreciate culture in terms of communities and as a process of passing down and shaping values within a local context, then the belief in the universality and neutrality of computer technologies will continue to perpetuate a fundamental misunderstanding of the colonizing and Westernizing impact of digitization on Iranian and other Muslim cultures.

Digitization is a form of colonization in the sense that it has embedded the assumptions of Western modernity, even as these assumptions are implicated in environment crises, the fracture of communities, the undermining of local traditions and the neglect of the dynamism of life. The assumption of computer science is that data accumulation and management is the key to solving problems, social and environmental, but in reality this is making those problems worse. Colonization proceeds in moving away from local cultures and traditions and towards global ones that are promoted as being universal. These abstract supposedly universal ideas undermine local tradition, though they are seductive because universal and abstract ideas lend themselves so well to print-based data management. Like other colonizing efforts, the global promotion of digitization entices local users with the prospect of progress, while reinforcing the cultural myths that overturn local traditions.

With the above overview as a framework of how digitization impacts culture, in the rest of this chapter we will illustrate these points in two ways. First, by looking in some detail at how digitization is debated and discussed by Iranian academics and policy makers, and by giving close attention to their explicit concerns and their implicit assumptions, we hope to demonstrate that their attention is entirely focused upon the promise and peril of digitization but that any understanding of the deeper cultural and ecological implications of digitization, as discussed above, is missing. Second, by considering in general a few widespread Islamic cultural traditions, we want to suggest how the voluntary adoption of digital technologies is altering and reshaping these traditions by moving them away from community and ecological relationships. The former illustration is important because it provides an insight into how academics and policy makers in the Muslim world are viewing digitization, while the latter illustration is important because the traditions mentioned, though altered, can also hold the key to cultural regeneration.

By analyzing the way that digital technologies are discussed in Iran, which is one of the cultural, economic, and political centers of the Muslim world today, we will attempt to demonstrate how the crucial cultural and ecological concerns related to digital technologies have been neglected. There are some reasons for this neglect. For the past decade, politics in Iran has been dominated by an ongoing struggle between conservatives and reformists, which impacts the way that digital technologies are discussed and understood. Conservatives see a threat in that information and communications technologies may question or limit their power, while for reformists they are often celebrated as a way to open up and share power. Both often claim benefits of using information technologies for economic development. However, when culture is evoked in discussions of digitization it is usually subservient to the dual focus on economics and politics. In many ways, there is a broad-based but unstated consensus in Iran regarding the adoption of digital technologies in that both sides to the ongoing debate are silent about the essential third dimension of culture.

Since the entrance of digital technologies into Iran, Islamic seminaries in the theological center of Qom have pioneered their adoption. These technologies, including software and databases, were mainly considered as neutral tools to facilitate access to, research on, and distribution of text-based theological resources. To organize these activities, the seminaries founded institutions and associations. One of the earliest was the Computer Research Center for Islamic Sciences (CRCIS), established in 1988 in Qom to digitize Islamic texts and sources. The ongoing activities of CRCIS include maintaining indices of Islamic sources to support research, using digital technologies to publish books and journals, providing computer training and services for researchers, cooperating with the computer industries to facilitate the goals of the Center, and utilizing the Internet to send and receive information. The CRCIS website states that its purpose is "to promote and develop the proper culture of computer usage and exchanging information within the Islamic seminaries, as well as recognizing and reinforcing the influential elements in this respect." A prominent producer of digital resources designed for Islamic studies is NoorSoft, which facilitates "access to Islamic texts using information and communication technologies and expanding these technologies in all of the Islamic seminary centers, domestically and internationally," as stated on their website (CRCIS, no date). NoorSoft produces software for use in "various fields of Islamic sciences and religious culture" and works to promote the "best methods of applying the Internet and intranets to send and receive the information required by researchers in the Islamic centers." Acting as a subsidiary to CRCIS, NoorSoft offers computer training and services designed to facilitate research, management, and distribution of the requisite information for Islamic studies. One of its overall goals, as noted in its mission statement, is "recognizing and enhancing the proper utilization of computer technology and then expanding it throughout the society."

The activities of Islamic seminaries in the field of information technologies are supported by Iran's supreme leader Ayatollah Khamenei, whose power is vested in his dual role as the highest political and religious authority of Iran. In a 1989 letter to CRCIS, penned after taking over the position of Supreme Leader upon the death of Imam Khomeini and referring to the highly revered family of the Twelve Imams of Shi'ism, Khamenei declared:

> Until the complete capacity of human creative thought is actualized, one cannot fully explore the divine knowledge and the depth of teachings of the Holy Family of Islam. These new technologies and tools are beneficial toward achieving this goal. You, as the skilled and knowledgeable youth,

ought to be thankful to God for being willing and able to use computers toward this goal, and you ought to continue this work for the sake of God and ask for His help to open the wellsprings of divine knowledge. I hope that your humble work will be accepted by God and that this new beginning will lead to an outcome of satisfaction and contentment.

With the blessings of the religious establishment in government, the theological centers remain the primary producers of software used for institutional as well as individual research purposes. However, it might be confusing and ironic to know that despite official support for such efforts, Iran has lagged behind the world in terms of access and speed of the Internet. This can be partly explained by the traditional approach of Islamic seminaries which, long before the digital age, considered knowledge as a valuable but nevertheless exclusive tool that should not be handed to or wielded by ordinary people for fear of misuse, and should be limited to specialists who know how to use it properly.

The technological infrastructure and public education facilities for usage of computers and the Internet remain limited in Iran due to conservative attitudes that see the Internet and virtual world as a perilous threat. This view reflects the usual conservative reaction toward any changes in the traditional attitudes and ways of life, but at the same time is mostly focused on the fear of losing the young generation to non-Islamic culture through viewing and participating in Western entertainment. This conservative reaction underlies policies for limiting Internet access and generally discouraging ordinary people from using it. The resulting political and socio-cultural disputes have contributed to Iran being ranked among the worst countries in terms of the quality and speed of the Internet. While the enacted policies may temporarily or partially limit access to digital entertainment and information, they do not recognize the deeper cultural and ecological impact of digitization, regardless of the content being transmitted. As we have been suggesting, digitization implicitly sorts knowledge into information that can be easily digitized and that which cannot, and by so doing has unwittingly redefined the meaning of knowledge.

Debates and discussions in Iran about digitization as a promise or a peril have been developing as computers have become more pervasive. A representative example, involving some of the prominent figures in information and communications technology in Iran today, was a debate on the topic of "the Internet as a threat or opportunity." Three academics specializing in information and communication technologies exchanged their views on the "new communication tools" and voiced concerns on how quickly the Iranian youth have embraced them. Published by the newspaper *Hamshahri* in June 2006, the debate demonstrates the way in which these technologies are discussed as a threat or an opportunity among Iranian academics. Illustrating the widespread view of technology as neutral, Hassan Namakdoust, a former professor of communications and head of the Hamshahri Research Institute, began the discussion by noting that computer technology in Iran "is used only as a communication tool, and there cannot be any threat involved with a communication tool." He continued: "Rather, a threat might emerge from content and contribution, which ought to be discussed as our weakness." He suggests that the discussion should be shifted to this weakness and how Iranians remain consumers of the content produced by others in cyberspace:

> How appropriate and up-to-date are the materials that we produce and contribute to cyberspace? This is what we should be worried about. The serious threat comes from obstacles in the way of producing diverse and appropriate content and the limitations that are put on such productions. If we don't produce, someone else will. We should not worry about what others produce; rather, we should worry about what we do not produce. The threat is that we observe but do not participate, and we consume but we do not produce.
>
> *(Hamshahri Online, June 26, 2006)*

Asked about why better advantage has not been taken of the Internet, in particular referring to the substandard and limited availability of connections, Namakdoust replied:

> Sometimes we forget that technology before everything is the child of its own time. Look at the Internet. How has it found its way into our lives? It was created when we wanted to share what we have with others. The Internet as a public phenomenon was created in the 1970s and 1980s when human beings arrived at a new meaning of life, our mental walls had fallen, we wanted to talk to each other, we were tired of the Cold War and social situations related to that, and had words to share with one another. However, we are threatened by the way we treat the technology, not by the technology itself.

Likening technology to a "newborn baby" that should not be judged until it has "grown up," Namakdoust embodies the common assumption of computer scientists in the West that digital technologies are merely neutral tools offering universal benefits of increased access to digitized information and that they facilitate communication, and what matters most is the social structure and conditions that govern the use of digital technologies. This view misses the crucial point that, quite apart from any implementation or use value, digital technologies have a profound impact on culture by sifting, sorting, and prioritizing one form of knowledge, that which is print based and easily digitized, over other forms of knowledge that are vernacular, experiential, and non-digitizable.

An opposing view, voiced by Professor of Computer Science Hosseini Pakdehi, holds that contributions are possible only when everyone is involved in control and ownership of the space, but that as long as the West owns and controls the Internet it remains a threat. Although an important observation, this is a recourse to the "digital divide" argument, which while disputing who can use the technology, does not question the belief in its non-neutrality. When Pakdehi notes that "technology is not neutral," this is evoked in the explicit sense of who built the Internet and controls access to it, which overlooks the question of the belief in the non-neutrality of technology as implicitly altering knowledge and relationships quite apart from who controls it or what is transmitted. Perpetuating the silence on the question of the non-neutrality of technology, Namakdoust dismisses Pakdehi's concern by stressing that even though control and ownership of information technology belongs to specific societies at present, it is possible to create the proper social conditions by which the digital divide can be bridged. Neither of these positions extend beyond the explicit meaning of neutrality as a political and economic concept, and therefore neglect the implicit belief in technology as a neutral tool that can simply be utilized toward whatever ends a society intends, which therefore does not extend into the deeper cultural and ecological implications.

The round table discussion concluded with Professor of Communication Sciences Dr. Shekarkhah observing that "in general there are two groups of ideas, those that are for and against technology, yet no one dares to claim that these technologies are not needed." They are needed, he insists, but what is important in the view of Shekarkhah is that communication and information technologies have not yet been properly institutionalized in Iranian society, that the requisite rules have not been set down for their use and that an Internet etiquette has not been developed. In a sense, he seems to be suggesting that Iranian society has not matured enough, perhaps even that it has not "caught up" with the West, to fully appreciate the value of information and communications technologies. While an important recognition of how technology can have a socio-cultural impact and even that its introduction changes cultural behaviors, this view still remains limited to the proper use of computers merely as neutral tools rather than recognizing the deeper cultural and ecological implications of adopting these tools.

The viewpoints expressed in the above debate are typical, and although expressed nearly a decade ago are remarkably similar to more recent viewpoints. For example, in 2012, the Association of Islamic Revolution Activists in Information Technology and Digital Media (ITDM) was established to determine the proper utilization of information technologies, the goal being "to organize a cultural front in cyberspace to promote the values and principles of the Islamic revolution" as well as to "combat the cultural attacks of the enemies of the Islamic Revolution" (2012). To ITDM, the digital world is a space similar to the real world, in which institutions need to use the appropriate tools and weapons to fight their enemies and to prove themselves. The ITDM director, Mehdi Sarami, noted in an interview with the conservative *Kayhan* newspaper on May 5, 2014 that digitization and the Internet strengthen the hegemony of the colonial powers and that the world is now facing a sort of virtual colonialism. However, like his colleagues above, Sarami believes that the tables can eventually be turned on the socio-political situation: "We don't believe that the virtual world has an essential tendency toward hegemonic powers; rather, the current situation is benefiting them. Therefore, we need to create a new order in which digital space is directed towards salvation, justice and progress" (May 5, 2014). While the power balances might be different, this "new order" would resemble the old order if the cultural and ecological implications of digitization are not recognized and addressed.

Reviewing the concerns regarding digitization, such as those outlined above, helps to see how they indicate a narrow view of culture and ecology, and illustrates the need for a deeper view of culture and ecology to fully understand the impact of technology and digitization. The discussions and debates have not moved beyond the polarization of promise and peril as understood primarily in terms of political and socio-economic concerns. Echoing the above viewpoints of the roundtable debate from 2006, Reza Gholami, head of the Sadra Research Center for Islamic Humanities, observed in an interview in June 2012 that the Internet included many kinds of data ranging from very dangerous to very useful. He stressed that since the West is the origin of this technology, most content and the best services have been produced and provided by the West and as a result the "decadent culture" of the West is dominant in the content and Western hegemony is dominant in the structure of the services provided. While using the Internet involves being directly or indirectly exposed to some aspects of Western culture, including scientific and economic achievements, to Gholami the Internet remains a perilous threat. However, he insists that it will one day be considered as an opportunity to send Islamic religious messages to the rest of the world without limitations, and all that is needed is the right infrastructure, as it is the strength of the infrastructure that can make the Internet more of an opportunity and less of a threat (Tabnak, June 6, 2012).

More recently, with the election of Hassan Rouhani as president of Iran, hopes were raised domestically and internationally that Iran's information and communications policies would be liberalized. President Rouhani publicly addressed the ongoing national debate on May 13, 2014, when he laid out his vision for a new approach in a speech at the Fourth National Festival of Information and Communication Technology. His views became a topic of intense national debate for some time thereafter. Rouhani criticized the conservative approach towards information and communication technologies, insisting that in the past "the world was moving towards a global village, but now it is moving towards a global family in which users are citizens" adding that "social media now have millions of users." Evoking Iran's heritage and the great poets of the past, as well as many of the hot button issues of the present, Rouhani continued by insisting:

> We should not look at the cyber world as a place that we entered due to urgency and desperation. Rather, we should consider it as an opportunity. In

an era that modern tools were not available, Hafiz, Saadi, Ferdowsi and Rumi honored the Iranian Islamic culture and handed it down to the next generations. Today a great space is available for the educated youth who love their country, especially female as well as male students in our universities, to honor the Iranian Islamic identity.

(Office of the President of the Islamic Republic of Iran, 2014)

Rouhani further emphasized Iran's need for creating knowledge-based industries and technologies not only for reasons of economic development and creating jobs, but also for developing public services and taking steps toward creating electronic government.

Rouhani's views were appreciated and became the subject of public discussion, as it was the first official stand against the dominant conservative attitude toward information and communications technologies. However, this has not yet gone beyond his words, as the government is still struggling with the budget needed to build and maintain the foundational infrastructure for high speed Internet access. While the goals may be laudable on the surface, focusing on increased and better provision of high speed Internet does not leave room for discussions of how digital technologies and the virtual world are colonizing society and how they are reshaping culture. At the same time, Rouhani adheres to the dominant pattern of promise by focusing on the access and distribution benefits of the digital technologies. While political activists might rightly applaud Rouhani's willingness to roll back some of the heavy handed and repressive tactics of his predecessor when it comes to freedom of speech, the pivotal questions of culture and ecology are left unaddressed and the current debates more or less reproduce previous debates, all of which remain unable to recognize the deeper cultural and ecological implications of digitization.

While there is of course some awareness of the cultural dimension of information and communication policy making, the focus is superficial and only on the cultural content being transmitted, which almost entirely emanates from print-based sources, whether religious or literary. This disregards the deeper ecological issues of how digitization itself is a culture-changing mechanism that sifts and sorts knowledge and experience and prioritizes that which can be easily digitized, namely texts, and undermines the rest. In spite of all the concerns about the limitations on the structure of technology used to spread superficial content, there is no deep understanding of the way digitization has changed culture regardless of differences in economic and political outlook. The cautious, and somewhat ironic, approach does not go beyond a fear of the agenda of the producers of Western technology in terms of the kind of content transmitted while embracing the possibility of controlling the Internet as a useful tool. While the embracing approach sees the information and communication technologies as neutral tools to be used for one's own agenda, it largely accepts this as an inevitable part of modern life, which is another indication of how awareness of the deeper cultural implications of computers is ignored or missing.

It is beyond the scope of this chapter to fully examine how academics and policy makers throughout the Muslim world understand the digital revolution, but the short case study on Iran as an important cultural center of the Muslim world can provide indications of how these issues are understood in other regions. We would like to therefore turn now to a more general discussion of cultural traditions in the Muslim world, surveying a number of community-based traditions that have already been undermined by computer technology. These traditions include sighting the moon to determine the ritual calendar for fasts, feasts, and pilgrimages, and knowing the position of the sun for the purpose of performing the daily ritual prayers. We will also briefly consider the impact of technology on calling the faithful to prayer, adding illumination and marginal comments to books, and approaching education through face-to-face communication. These traditions were selected not only because they are being undermined, but also because their widespread and contemporary relevance in Muslim communities positions them to hold the potential for cultural regeneration.

Central elements of Islamic ritual practice are determined by observing the sun and moon. The times for daily ritual and communal prayers are based on the position of the sun at sunrise, noon, and sunset. The lunar-based Islamic calendar informs the timing of important communal rituals, such as concluding the Ramadan fast or commencing the pilgrimage to Mecca. In the past, attention to determining the accurate timings of ritual practices led to several groundbreaking developments in astronomy. The observations of Muslim astronomers, while looking toward the sky, kept people grounded on the earth through their purpose of supporting ritual practice. This stands in marked distinction compared to the way astronomy has developed in the West, as a tool for space travel and searching for interplanetary resources. While it is still possible to determine the timings for rituals through skilled observation, as was done in the past, these are largely prescribed today through the use of mathematical tables that can predict the timing and dates of rituals well into the future, thus obviating the need for any sort of physical observation. Reliance on instantaneous electronic and digital communication has only worsened the problem, as now what used to be a locally determined ritual practice is subject to verification by authorities far away from the locale. This is further confused by competition among states and sects to be the first to proclaim the end of the Ramadan fast, which instead of being applicable to the locality in which the moon can actually be sighted now occurs on a planetary scale but is subjected to the whims of regional political systems.

As we saw with the Iranian policy makers above, who are by no means alone in their viewpoints, it is as if Western modernity is inevitably penetrating all aspects of life and all that can be done is to align the local culture and lifestyle with it. This has already been occurring in the Muslim world with previous technological change. For example, the call to prayer, an essential element of community gathering and ritual expression that relies on a well-trained human voice in a close-knit social context within earshot, was already being replaced, beginning in the 1960s with the advent of audio recording and sound amplification technologies. The human relationships supporting these ritual practices are being further marginalized by computer software and digital clocks that separate people from traditions by announcing the prayer time on personal computers, digital watches, and other electronic gadgets that are increasingly adopted by isolated individuals sitting at their office desks or playing with their smart phones in bed. The traditional vocal art of the call to prayer has become deskilled through the reliance on recordings, some made decades ago, that are now further removed through digitization. The increasing reliance on a mediated and digitized call to prayer severs relationships and reduces an important tradition to the element of fulfilling an individual religious ritual, which is undermining the social aspects and communal basis of those rituals. In the past, physically observing the sun and moon kept people in touch with nature; today we can only "observe" nature as mediated by mathematical tables and computer screens.

The digitization of culture and the particular worldview embedded in digital technologies are an extension of the reliance on print-based media. These come together with the ascendancy of electronic books and other media that recreate but further abstract print-based knowledge. While print-based media have already alienated knowledge from its cultural and ecological contexts, digitizing these media further removes them from the lived realities of physical books. Muslims routinely refer to themselves, along with Jews and Christians, as "people of the book," yet seem unaware that digitization sacrifices vibrant long standing traditions of a culture with deep respect for books. For example, in digitizing books an entire craft-based culture is lost, which in the Muslim world, as well as in other cultures, has a long and diverse history in the form of illumination of the printed word and through writing marginal comments on pages, both of which evoke various times and places through the tactile elements still embedded in books. Digitization creates an ephemeral abstract world of free-floating information detached from people and places that makes all books look the same and reduces the reading experience to the uniform scanning of electronic texts.

Like their counterparts the world over, advocates of digitization in the Muslim world refer to the promise of expanding interaction and increasing access to information for the purpose of teaching and learning and passing down traditions. While it is true that, especially in the past two decades, there has been a proliferation of interactive education based on discussion around shared interests, these have come almost entirely at the expense of the face-to-face communication that has driven most forms of education for centuries. Given this history, it is in some ways illusory and even delusional to see a proliferation of online education as evidence of increased learning and the maintaining of cultural traditions. It ignores the potentially adverse impact that this might have on the kind of communication that can only come about within face-to-face interactions that are rooted in communities. The well-meaning advocacy of diversifying access and increasing the distribution of learning materials assumes that digitization is neutral

and holds great promise for learning. However, what remains less well understood is how digital technologies separate learning from lived realities and the
unintended consequences of assuming that digital information is merely an
extension of culturally grounded knowledge. Digitization by its very nature
excludes forms of knowledge that cannot be represented by bits and bytes, and in
so doing has redefined knowledge itself as only that which can be digitized.
While online education may help to manage and monetize teaching and learning,
it also reinvents the learning process as technologically mediated communication
with people who we may not really know beyond their screen personas, or who
may not even be present on the other side of the computer as their lectures and
lessons are digitized. In this way, online education is replacing, rather than
extending, face-to-face learning.

The Muslim community-based and historically grounded rituals and traditions
noted above are in danger of being abandoned through increasing reliance on
technology and its deskilling effects, as human interactions have largely been
replaced or mediated by interactions with machines and data. In turn, these
interactions with data have made local forms of authority, interpretation, and
determination of ritual timings and calendars subject to global authorities. However, given the cultural significance and long history of these rituals and traditions, it is still possible to regenerate them in ways that support diversity, locality,
and community. Owing to the differences in the way the moon and sun are
experienced in various locales and at different times of the year, it is almost as if
the Islamic tradition has a built-in protective feature that urges believers to keep
part of their consciousness focused on natural cycles and systems. While these
cycles and systems have not been altered, human perceptions of them have, so it
is a matter of re-orienting perceptions of rituals and traditions back to the local
natural features and away from the global technological industries. There is no
need to text or email distant authorities to see if the moon has been sighted when
it can be easily sighted in a locale, and there is no need to proclaim a planetary
fast when it is entirely feasible to participate in fasting and feasting within the
immediate locale. What matters is carrying out the rituals and traditions in face-
to-face community settings that bring people together and these can still be just as
easily, and probably more healthily, carried out in any particular locale.

Digital technologies have had an especially deskilling effect on the visual and
audio arts, but these, too, can be regenerated by a reorientation away from
machines and data and more toward the human communities that they are
intended to serve. While it might be edifying to listen to a beautiful iconic
recording of the call to prayer made in Cairo in the 1960s, it is also possible to
develop this vocal art in a locality today, and since there are various ways of
offering it with varying degrees of musicality, actually performing the call to
prayer in person can also become an expression of local sound arts. Similarly,
while it is more convenient to mass produce books, this in a way decreases the
respect for the written word that comes about when books are painstakingly

created, decorated, and annotated by hand. Digital typesetting normalizes and then mass produces certain fonts and cursive styles at the expense of others, acclimating culture and behavior to the uniform conveniences of industrialized production and distribution. However, it is still possible to regenerate the aesthetic sensibilities and preferences that proceed from and respond to the inherent diversity in chanting and writing as local cultural practices. In many ways, education is at the core of all these regenerations, if we extend education beyond its current fixation on interacting with machines and data in schools and reclaim the potential of education as a form of awareness that proceeds from and responds to the inherent diversity of traditional cultures that remain rooted in community and nature.

6

A DIFFERENT KIND OF CONNECTIVITY

How we understand the world, either as fixed, isolated, and thus as made up of autonomous entities or as emergent, relational, and interdependent, is critical to understanding the current problems posed by the globalization of the digital revolution. Beyond the problem of reducing the complex ecologies that underlie what we so casually refer to as knowledge, there is the problem of whether there will be any place for different cultural traditions of wisdom and moral values as data, the decision-making programs of computer experts, and the Western myth of the autonomous (that is, self-centered) individual become more widespread.

To Summarize How the Emphasis on Data Reduces Human Experience

Data can be useful in understanding past and current behaviors, and even in predicting future developments if one is willing to overlook the inherent limitations of data as well as the culturally specific interpretative frameworks that define what constitutes data—including how it should be used. To restate the most critical issue about the limitations of data: data is acquired through technologies that observe and measure a segment of a behavior or an event, and thus what occurs at a specific moment in time. The ability to rapidly observe and record a series of behaviors and events creates the impression that the data provides a full and accurate account. But the data, in reality, provides only a momentary account of the emergent and interdependent relationships that are the guiding forces within the natural ecology or largely by taken for granted cultural patterns. The latter includes the moral values encoded in the language that influences reflective decision making, in the taken for granted traditions upon which the cultural commons depends, and the internal states of consciousness of the person whose behavior is being observed and recorded. The internal states may include a keen sense of maintaining high personal standards of craftsmanship, in doing just enough to get by, and a multitude of other attitudes, values, memories, and identity issues that the data cannot reveal. Biographical distinct histories, along with a mix of taken for granted cultural patterns, are always part of what drives personal motivation that is beyond the reach of data collecting technologies and the new breed of data scientists who are not aware of the cultural and natural ecologies from which the data is extracted. And there is also the widely unrecognized way in which many of our metaphors encode the moral values of earlier eras and are reproduced today in thinking about the behavioral and policy strategies that data supports. For example, the earlier analogs that framed the meaning of such metaphors as women, traditions, and weeds, depending upon the culture, encoded what was assumed to be the appropriate moral behaviors. It was (and still is) morally appropriate to compensate woman less than men, to overturn traditions in order to build something new, and to use pesticides on weeds. Even the silence that is fostered by the emphasis on data as the source of knowledge involves unrecognized moral issues.

It is the limited sequence and still surface snapshots of a behavior that is part of a cultural ecology of emergent human relationships, which also involve interdependent relationships and information exchanges with the natural ecologies, that reveals the limitations of data. The limitations also include the interpretative frameworks (ideologies) of the people who make policy decisions based on the data, and how it is to be used. Most have undergone a university education that reinforced the Enlightenment misconceptions about the nature of cultural traditions, leaving them largely unaware of how the vocabulary they take for granted is based on the metaphorical thinking of earlier cultural eras—and unaware of the scientific bias that there is such a thing as an objective (that is, culture-free) way of knowing. Their university education will have left them with the same taken for granted deep cultural assumptions about individualism, progress, a mechanistic and human centered world, and a combination of hubris and messianic drive to impose their way of thinking on the rest of the world. If this description of the experts who now claim the ability to turn their interpretation of the data into predictions of the future has a familiar ring it is because the computer scientists and their hyper-motivated army of supporters underwent a similar educational experience—often at our most elite universities. What is universally shared within the emerging data-driven culture is the lack of awareness that data cannot provide an account of the full range of historical influences on what is being observed and measured. Furthermore, the data cannot escape being interpreted by experts who are unlikely to be aware of the cultural assumptions that have influenced their own thinking and values.

Data, for example, cannot reveal how the ethnic background of a student, such as coming from an oral culture, might lead to a lower performance on a print-based computer-scored test. It might lead to recognizing a correlation that reveals lower test scores of other members of a predominately oral culture. But it obscures the more important issues such as how learning about the abstract world of a print-based curriculum may be regarded as less useful than what is learned from the combination of place-based skills and knowledge shared orally and in mentoring relationships. The issues become even more complicated when the place-based sharing of intergenerational knowledge and skills has a smaller adverse impact on natural systems than the print-based curriculum that reinforces the deep cultural assumptions about individualism, progress, a human-centered world, and moving up as high as possible on the pyramid of consumerism. As will be explained later, learning the intergenerational knowledge and skills within the cultural commons, whether it's the cultural commons within some cultural segment of mainstream America or that of an ethnic or indigenous group, has little use for data—even though they may find the Internet useful in connecting with each other and with the wider world.

Data is highly useful in learning how different cultural lifestyles impact natural systems. But it is also complicit in exacerbating the market-driven forces accelerating the growth of the economy that is changing the chemistry of the world's oceans, and thus weather systems that are leading to droughts, shortage of water, and changes in habitats. The values at the center of these market forces include the drive to achieve greater efficiency, the centralization of power and control, and greater profits. These values are central to the Common Core Curriculum promoted by industry leaders such as Rex Tillerson (Chairman of the Board and CEO of ExxonMobil) and Bill Gates, as well as politicians across the country. These values are just as central to the efforts of computer scientists and engineers to replace workers with robots and computer systems. Collecting data on people's performance, whether on an assembly line, in the operating room where more computer systems are replacing the traditional role and skills of surgeons, in a myriad of other work settings that involve a high degree of routine procedures, provides what is misrepresented as objective data that justifies replacing humans with machines. Who can question the values of improved efficiency and profits, especially if one stands outside a system that is unresponsive to being questioned?

How Big Data and Big Profits Replace Wisdom

Cisco, a leader in the growing field of networking technologies, recently announced that the use of sensors and actuators connecting objects and things in the Internet of Everything would become over the next 10 years a 19 billion dollar global market. Wireless connectivity, estimated to introduce between 24 and 30 billion devices over the next half decade, will include smart thermostats and household refrigerators and washer/dryers, biochip transponders in humans and animals, sensors in cars and trucks, and monitoring (that is data collecting) devices that will connect children to their parents and everything to everything. This data will be stored in the massive data centers now referred to as the cloud and used by the new breed of data analysts to predict market trends. During times of social crises it will also be made available to government agencies, including the police and other law enforcement agencies tasked with suppressing dissent as the technologically displaced workers and the ecological crises deepen.

In the same way the Internet is now altering the consciousness of the digital generation that has grown up focused on digital screens and experiencing the phenomenon of instantaneous access on the Internet, the amount of data collected and stored from the increased scale of surveillance and connectivity will further undermine such old traditions as the narratives, ceremonies, and the people recognized as the keepers of a culture's wisdom. Indeed, as the metaphors of "information" and "data" have taken on more importance, wisdom has disappeared from the vocabulary of the users and promoters of digital technologies. This raises a special problem in cultures that have not been so overwhelmed with poverty and racked by extremists that their wisdom traditions have disappeared entirely. As they are also scheduled to part of the 24 to 30 billion dollar market of connecting everything to everything, their youth, like the youth in Westernized cultures, will become first indifferent to the wisdom traditions of their older generations and then pulled into the ranks of extremists as the material world encountered on the digital screens remains out of reach.

While the digital revolution is hostile toward all wisdom traditions, it is driven by a specific set of Western values. As values are integral to moral decisions that govern the emergent and relational world in which we live, it is important to identify how values frame the nature of what in the past was understood as the moral codes that should govern relationships. Values such as integrity, fairness, respect, and so forth were, in our recent past, thought to be the basis of moral decisions guiding relationships with others. As we know from daily experience values guiding decisions about relationships also may be exploitive, such as valuing profits over concerns about the fate of the worker, valuing a consumer lifestyle over that of an ecologically sustainable future, valuing the experience of killing an animal even though its species is headed to extinction. Values are often subjectively and culturally influenced, and may have nothing to do with what was regarded in the past as moral decisions. Almost everything the computer futurists predict, including how super computers will lead to the extinction of organic life (including humans), is based on instrumental values influenced by the culturally and historically influenced metaphorical language that is the taken for granted basis of their thinking. Efficiency, convenience, progress, connectivity, profits, abundance, data, freedom, virtual reality, and so forth, are all valued by computer scientists and the growing culture of technological and market-driven innovators.

As many Americans share these values, they also assume that computer scientists are promoting what is important to them. This correspondence in thinking about what to value can be seen in how few Americans are raising moral concerns about the development of total surveillance systems that now make privacy a thing of the past, the loss of employment as the workplace becomes increasingly computerized, the ability of people to be judged guilty and thus unemployable on the basis of what they may have read in an online course that can be monitored by a potential employer. The collective silence also extends to the moral issues related to the ways in which computers contribute to the colonization of other cultures, and to the loss of intergenerational knowledge and skills that strengthen the mutual support systems within communities. The distinction between values and moral decisions needs to be considered in the following discussion of how the emphasis on data, and other forms of electronic cultural storage and communication, marginalizes the importance of moral decisions.

Cultural values that emphasize achieving more efficiency, increasing profits, adopting newer technologies that replace workers, and moving decision making to the top of the workplace hierarchy support the scientific/corporate mindset of the digital culture. It is not clear whether Kurzweil is thinking as a scientist or as Darwin's oracle when he claims that as the world enters the era of singularity super computers will not only displace humans in the evolutionary process, but will also have religious experiences that will provide the moral guidelines for the new world order. I strongly suspect that few of his colleagues and even fewer scientists take his prediction seriously. Yet, his way of thinking of a world of data-based decision making and where moral decisions are being replaced by the forces of evolution, as E. O. Wilson, Richard Dawkins, and others are now arguing, is not too different from the capitalist's moral code that promotes decisions where the values of profits and power displace decisions that take account of the well-being of the Other—which may be a person or the environment.

For example, data on increases in efficiency and profits is now used as the basis for replacing workers with robots. This is an example of how data now bypasses human and nature-centered moral systems. Similarly, what are the arguments used to justify the near total surveillance systems that now exist at all levels of American society? Today, collecting data on people's behaviors and on what they are thinking (which is the new technological frontier computer scientists are now working on) is not being discussed as a moral issue, which it is. It would be useful to learn about the vocabulary used by the people running the technologies of the National Security Agency and other intelligence agencies to explain to themselves and others why they collect, without a warrant, the data on people's lives. Do they use any words (metaphors) that suggest they are aware of moral issues? Or is it a political/police-state vocabulary where the collection of data is understood as the basis of power and control over a population that may harbor radical ideas?

Historically, the cultural changes that led to the adoption of civil rights were originally the outcome of moral/religious narratives, but the growing attrition of historical memory is leading to the loss of a moral vocabulary—except in some social justice-oriented churches and among minority groups attempting to be heard above the noise of the Kafkaesque data keepers. The old vocabulary used in sorting out the differences between moral and immoral behavior, such as in the treatment of marginalized groups, in addressing social justice issues in the workplace, and in human/Nature relationships, seems increasingly dated in a world where data (and now Big Data) has been elevated to a special status. Words and phrases such as "dignity," "humane," "respect," "do unto others as you would have them do unto you," and so forth, seem to be slipping into the realm of silence that accompanies the digital revolution—with its emphasis on personal conveniences, efficiency in the workplace, and consumerism.

"Progress" is another word that is marginalizing the possibility of a national moral discourse about who benefits from the social practices that relegate millions of children and adults to a life of homelessness, hunger, and insecurity. If the huge inequality in the distribution of wealth in America, where the top 1 percent of the population owns nearly 40 percent of the nation's wealth, is a result of progress—who is prepared to question progress? How many Americans possess the conceptual background necessary for questioning an abstraction such as "progress"?

It is important to recognize that while the average person on the street still attempts to reconcile the transcendent moral codes that can be traced back to religious traditions and mythopoetic narratives with the competing demands of a consumer culture, it is the governing elites in business, education, agriculture, politics, and the media that have now elevated data to the ultimate and final basis for their decisions. Data (and profits) now plays the central role in determining which innovations are to define the norms others are to embrace. It's not the depth of insights and wisdom about human/Nature relationships acquired over decades of experience—which are examples of the cultural commons. Rather, data-based decision making reduces the importance of considering earlier influences—especially those that enabled people to live less consumer-dependent lives.

In the field of education, for example, the student is scored on tests and the data collected on the students' behavior, and not on how their education leads to important social contributions in the future. What is being lost are the judgments based on what is learned in face-to-face relationships, which often involve insights evaluated and refined over many generations. And given the complex and interdependent cultural ecologies within which face-to-face relationships take place, there are few decisions that are not based on tacitly held moral values.

Just as print marginalizes awareness of the complexity of what is being communicated in face-to-face relationships, as well as the personal memories that may be the basis for empathy and even altruistic responses, decisions based on data limit awareness of the well-being of the Other. People can be dismissed from their jobs with no thought given to their special circumstance that might preclude them obtaining another job or being able to feed themselves and educate their children. Over-reliance upon data and objectifying technologies such as print depersonalize communication, as in the case of bullying. Face-to-face bullying involves being immediately accountable (which may not make a difference for some people). The abstract encounter, whether in the form of data and even photographs (with only a few exceptions due to the special talent of the photographer), diminishes attention given to the plight of the Other as other information and images compete for attention. When repeated over and over, data on the billions of people living on less than two dollars a day can have the same impact as learning about the upcoming week's weather forecast. The abstract nature of data desensitizes and thus contributes to adopting an objective and indifferent stance toward the Other.

Social justice movements, whether they addressed the exploitation of child labor, migrant workers, social groups deemed inferior, or the destruction of natural systems, have been motivated by the insights of people rooted in different moral traditions of thinking and acting—ranging from Susan B. Anthony, John Muir, Mahatma Gandhi, to Martin Luther King Jr. Civil society, whether on a street corner, playground, or at a public meeting, depends upon people exercising moral judgments about what will improve the fairness and well-being of others. Outside of the social venues where data-based decision making has become the primary focus, most people make moral decisions with data being a secondary concern. For Schmidt and Cohen, the people who have not made data their primary concern are not fully connected to the *New Digital Age* (that is) *Reshaping the Future*, as they put it. Just as Ayn Rand made the rational pursuit of self-interest the ultimate goal, the computer scientists are turning data into the ultimate form of knowledge that is to be the basis of human decision making.

One of the current efforts to reshape the future is the research now being done by computer scientists to create what are being called "robot warriors" that can function as autonomous weapons systems. These systems can be programmed so that humans are not required to be part of the decision-making process. Again, the ability to collect data on the enemy and the terrain, and to use it to aim the weapons systems, will change the nature and likely frequency of warfare— especially as there are now 76 countries conducting military robotics research and development. It will be interesting to see whether computer scientists raise moral concerns similar to the moral stance taken by an earlier generation of scientists concerned with the proliferation of nuclear weapons. Or will they view this line of research and development as another opportunity to demonstrate the transformative potential of digital technologies?

Impact of the Digital Revolution on the Moral and Wisdom Traditions of Other Cultures

As digitally mediated storage, thinking, and communication become increasingly dominant, other linguistic/cultural ecologies that rely on narratives, ceremonies, communal memories of social justice struggles, elder knowledge of human/ Nature relationships, and stories of origins that also establish what should be regarded as sacred, are receding from conscious awareness. But even in North

America, these alternative linguistic/cultural ecologies still exist, but are coming under increasing pressure as the youth are increasingly pulled into the seemingly limitless freedoms of cyberspace. What is important about these traditions of the cultural commons is not a concern of the computer scientists who are focused on transforming not only Western cultures, but the world's other cultures. Given their indifference to learning about their own cultural traditions, especially those that strengthen the self-sufficiency of local communities, it is doubtful that many proponents of the digital revolution have heard of the cultural commons—even though they tacitly rely upon them as sources of meaning, skills, and family connectedness. The cultural commons represent the face-to-face and inter-generational gift economy that cannot be digitized because of its taken for granted status in daily experience.

The other important question today, beyond that of how the abstract and superficially connected world of data-based decision making is relegating the old-fashioned traditions of moral reciprocity to the past that evolution is now moving beyond, is whether the globalization of the digital revolution will undermine what remains of the wisdom traditions of non-Western culture that provide different pathways to morally coherent and community-centered lives. One of the achievements of these varied wisdom traditions is that they enabled people to avoid the pursuit of instant self-gratification, the relentless drive for personal wealth, competitive individualism, exploitation of the environment, and a moral indifference to the plight of others. However, what we are now witnessing in many non-Western countries is how their national development plans are contingent upon adopting more digital technologies and creating a consumer-oriented middle class that will live by the individually centered values that the culture's wisdom traditions previously held in check—especially the expectation of instant gratification.

Wisdom traditions have often been too challenging for people to fully adhere to, and the regions of the world where they originated and continue to have the greatest number of followers have not been free of wars of aggression and horrendous treatment of those regarded as inferior or as outsiders. So the question of how the digital revolution will impact what remains of these wisdom traditions, which hundreds of millions of older people are still attempting to live by, should not be framed in terms of dichotomous categories. Rather, the questions needing to be addressed are: (1) Will the global spread of the print- and the data-based cultural epistemology that accompanies the digital revolution lead the youth of these cultures to achieve a balance between their culture's wisdom traditions and the West's emphasis on possessive individualism? (2) Can Google and similar websites provide the youth in these regions an understanding of different wisdom traditions such as Buddhism, Confucianism, and those of indigenous cultures? Or, are these wisdom traditions renewed primarily through face-to-face communication and mentoring relationships and thus likely to be lost to the new digital modes of communication? (3) Have digital technologies shortened people's attention spans (particularly that of youth) to the point where issues such as climate change, computerization of the workplace, and the loss of the cultural commons have ceased to have more than a momentary interest? (4) As digital technologies and the media now make it possible to exist only in communities of shared interest, will they lead to replacing the old democratic value of diversity with the value of an ideologically driven conformity—and intolerance for the Other?

Neither awareness of the importance of wisdom traditions nor awareness of the cultural forces contributing to the ecological crisis have altered the thinking of the computer futurist writers. Peter Diamandis and Steven Kotler, for example, write in the sub-section of *Abundance* about "This Moaning Pessimism" of environmentalists (2012, 38–40). It would seem that the computer scientists working with environmental scientists would be aware of the silence in the thinking of the computer futurist writers, and would initiate a critical discussion about whether the computer futurist's combination of extreme optimism about the future and the Social Darwinian scenario of how humans will be replaced by super computers reflects losing touch with today's realities. But then the ecologically informed computer scientists may also be victims of their own narrow educational backgrounds, and thus lack ideas about the cultural transformations that must be undertaken beyond what has now become a formulaic response about the need for new technologies that will slow the rate of environmental degradation. It is highly probable that their education did not include thinking about the ecological importance of the wisdom traditions that were part of the cultural commons that have guided people's lives before governments, technologies, and economic resources were used to create the myth of unending progress.

How computer futurist thinkers, as well as other proponents of the digital revolution, represent the nature of wisdom is also important to consider, as their narrow understanding has implications as to whether they are conceptually able to help the public understand the limitations of digitally mediated thinking and communication. Helping other cultures, especially those now embracing the Western model of economic and technological development and modernization, to understand the traditions that will be sacrificed on the altar of modernization will become more critical as sources of water, protein, and livable habitats come under greater stress.

Wisdom traditions that go back thousands of years are not mentioned, except by the Social Darwinian computer futurists who have announced that natural selection has relegated them to the list of upcoming extinctions. The word "wisdom" is still part of the vocabulary of Schmidt and Cohen, but they use it in a way that associates the word with the prevailing crowd mentality. As they put it, "collective wisdom on the Internet is a controversial subject," with some associating it with the "hive mind" while others associate it with the "accuracy and reliability of crowd sourced information platforms such as Wikipedia" (2013, 197).

This brief description of wisdom is important as it reveals how the word, which encompasses the major part of humankind's moral legacy, is now being reduced to information and data. If this understanding of wisdom prevails among the generation that has come of age using digital technologies, there will be a huge loss both for themselves and for the cultures being colonized by the promotion of the digital/market/consumer-oriented culture. Even a surface understanding of the wisdom traditions of other cultures would be useful in becoming aware of what remains of the wisdom traditions within the different cultural ecologies we call America. It needs to be recognized that undermining the wisdom traditions of non-Western cultures will have an even greater impact on natural systems that will lead to catastrophic social consequences. Many of these wisdom traditions were, and continue to be for some indigenous cultures, the basis for mentoring youth in how to live a mindful existence and to take responsibility for the well-being of the environment and future generations.

Among the oldest wisdom traditions in the world are those of the Aboriginal peoples who occupied for tens of thousands of years what is now called Australia. As many in the West regard Aboriginal peoples as among the most "primitive" of the world, the question becomes: should their voices be taken seriously about whether they want their children raised as citizens of the New Digital Age, as Schmidt and Cohen refer to it?

Deborah Bird Rose, an American ethnographer who lived for years among the Yarralin people, summarized the transcendent rules that aligned their thoughts, feelings, and actions in the present with their shared cosmology of the eternal "Creation Time" (or Dream Time):

- **Balance**: A system cannot be life enhancing if it is out of kilter, and each part shares in the responsibility of sustaining itself and balancing others.
- **Response**: Communication is reciprocal. There is a moral obligation: to learn to understand, to pay attention, and to respond.
- **Symmetry**: In opposing and balancing each other, parts must be equivalent because the purpose is not to 'win' or to dominate, but to block, thereby producing further balance.
- **Autonomy**: No species, no group, or country is boss of another, each adheres to its own Law. Authority and dependence are necessary within parts, but not between parts.

(Suzuki and Knudtson, 1992, 47)

These moral guidelines were understood for thousands of years before Gregory Bateson, one of the most important thinkers of our times, articulated a similar set of guidelines for living in an emergent, relational, and interdependent world. As he put it:

"Thus, in no system which shows mental characteristics can any part have unilateral control over the whole. In other words, *the mental characteristics of the system are immanent, not in some part, but in the system as a whole*" (italics in the original, 1972, 316).

By mental characteristics, he meant any form of communication that occurs in the relational worlds of cultural and environmental ecologies. In other words, life in its multiple dimensions depends upon communication, with each species being dependent upon its unique semiotic capacity for multiple information exchanges with other systems. In effect, the emergent and relational characteristics of all cultural and natural ecologies are cognitive systems.

Indigenous cultures in different regions of the world have also developed and lived by wisdom traditions from which we can learn—which is different than copying them. Their wisdom traditions represent the moral guidelines that govern relationships and interdependencies within the cultural and natural ecological systems that contemporary scientists are just beginning to understand. Moreover, these traditions are intergenerationally passed forward through face-to-face and mentoring relationships. This leads to the multidimensional process of learning where all the senses are involved, as well as learning to give close attention to the behavior (that is, communication patterns) of plants and animals. There are also ceremonies and rituals that further reinforce awareness of the interdependencies between cultural practices and the natural ecologies.

The influence of wisdom traditions on daily practices can be seen in the following examples of indigenous cultures:

> Survival based on hunting requires an intimate knowledge of the behavior, habitat and seasonal preferences of animals. It also requires knowledge of their reproductive patterns. Awareness of participating in a sacred universe requires adhering to moral protocols in tracking and killing of an animal. Part of the moral code requires killing only what is needed, and not killing for fun or to demonstrate personal power and ability.
>
> (Statement by Hopi religious leaders) This land was granted to the Hopi by a power greater than man can explain. Title is invested in the whole make-up of Hopi life. Everything is dependent upon it. The land is sacred and if the land is abused, the sacredness of Hopi life will disappear and all other life as well.
>
> (Wisdom traditions that separate the Wintu of Northern California from the colonizing Western culture) When we Indians kill meat, we eat it all up. When we dig roots we make little holes. When we build houses, we make little holes. When we burn grass for grasshoppers we don't ruin things. We shake down acorns and pine nuts. We don't cut down the trees. We only use dead wood. But the white man plows up the ground, pulls up the trees, kills everything … When Indians use rocks they take little round ones for cooking. The white people dig deep tunnels. They make roads. They dig as much as they wish. They don't care how much the ground cries out …
>
> *(Suzuki and Knudtson, 1992, 99, 169, 201–202)*

The wisdom traditions of different indigenous cultures reflect a profoundly different way of thinking than what we find in the writings of the computer futurist writers, and in the thinking of computer scientists in search of how human behaviors and tasks can be replaced by digital technologies. The vocabularies of indigenous cultures—which evolved over thousands of years of giving careful attention to their interdependent relationship with animals, the land, and the yearly cycles of renewal—are the basis of highly developed forms of ecological intelligence. They reflect an awareness of participation in a larger reality that both nourishes and requires responsible (that is, moral) behavior that both conserves and intergenerationally renews what is in effect a land ethic. The English equivalent vocabulary includes "humility," "reverence," "compassion," "generosity," "sacred," and "self-limitation." The pathology of hubris is noticeably absent. The field of computer science, which is not lacking in generosity in meeting the needs of others, derives its progress-oriented vocabulary from the scientific, technological, and profit-driven industrial culture.

When various wisdom vocabularies are understood as verbs rather than nouns that limit awareness of the relational and emergent world that characterizes all forms of life, we confront the deepest and ecologically most important aspects of human experience that cannot be represented on a computer screen other than as abstractions. Describing these experiences requires a vocabulary that refers to moral awareness of relationships that are not exploitive, non-competitive, and non-monetized. The question that needs to be asked is whether these moral values can be learned on the Internet or from educational software programs. Or is a mentoring relationship required for youth to learn how to translate the moral vocabulary derived from a wisdom tradition into their behaviors toward the Other? Do mentoring relationships help to solidify a self-concept of being a morally responsible person—or are youth to be left to their own subjective insights and feelings as currently promoted by many American educators? It is important to note that the UNESCO agenda of promoting global educational reforms that foster sustainable thinking also echoes the American tradition of promoting the student's self-discovery and construction of knowledge.

What is important about the wisdom traditions of many indigenous cultures is that leading scientists such as George Wald (Nobel Prize winning biologist), Stephen J. Gould (evolutionary biologist), John Platt (biophysicist), Roger Sperry (Nobel Prize winning neurobiologist), Aldo Leopold (ecologist), Ilya Prigogine (Nobel Prize winning physicist), among others, recognize the parallels between the various wisdom traditions and the exercise of ecological intelligence that is devoid of the hubris so prevalent among Western thinkers.

Unfortunately, just as the world's diversity of spoken languages is disappearing from the pressures of modernization, the world's wisdom traditions are also under threat from the same forces. Perhaps the greatest source of threat is in how digital technologies are undermining the intergenerational communication, thus cutting youth off from the forms of knowledge that cannot be reduced to data or adequately represented in print. As pointed out earlier, what appears on the computer screen encodes the thought processes, including the deep taken for granted cultural assumptions, of the people who collected the data or framed the sequences of a computer-mediated learning experience. The power of the abstract world they create as well as the exciting visual images and performances appearing on the computer screen shape personalities and self-identities in ways that are less aware of the relational and interdependent world in which they are situated. Perhaps most important of all, given the rapidly degraded state of natural systems, is that the students will not experience the sacred—and the range of embodied moral relationships that extend to the non-human world.

The insight contained in The Haudenosauneethe Declaration of the Iroquois points to the fundamental truth that all uses of digital technologies should be judged by: "*We who walk about on Mother Earth occupy this place for only a short time. It is our duty as human beings to preserve the life that is here for the benefit of generations yet unborn*" (Suzuki and Knudtson, 1992, 240). The only qualification that needs to be made is the reference to "generations yet unborn," which should be understood as including the non-human world.

Given that what remains of the world's diverse wisdom traditions promotes, among other values, an environmental ethic, and given the efforts of computer scientists to globalize a technology that is not culturally neutral but reinforces an instrumental and market understanding of life, there are a number of important questions that need to be raised: (1) Can the world's ecosystems survive what Schmidt and Cohen envision as the next stage of progress; namely the Westernization of five billion people who will, in becoming connected to the Internet, lose their largely non-monetized cultural commons lifestyles? (2) Will access to scientific reports, computer models of life-altering changes in the world's ecosystems, such as the melting of the continental ice sheet that covers Antarctica, and to the massive amounts of data on the loss of habitats and species (including the world's fisheries) lead to the same restraints on human behavior as the wisdom traditions of the world? (3) Is the failure to submit the digital revolution to some form of a democratic process in non-Western countries contributing to the violent resistance to being colonized by technologies that are based on Western values and ways of thinking?

For example, fundamental differences between the cultural patterns reinforced by print- and data-based storage, thinking, and communication can be seen by comparing the difference between what the Buddhist call the Path, and what they refer to as "wandering about"—which refers to the lifestyle that is not reflective and thus is continually influenced by outside forces and shifting subjective whims. The lifestyle of "wandering about" is exemplified in the West as a consumer-driven lifestyle and the many illnesses that accompany it.

The Path, on the other hand, leads to a lifestyle of mindfulness and thus to a radical transformation in life's guiding principles. The Path's eight steps include the following: (1) Right views, (2) Right Intent, (3) Right Speech, (4) Right

Conduct, (5) Right Livelihood, (6) Right Effort, (7) Right Mindfulness, (8) Right Concentration (Smith, 1991, 105–112). It is notable that possessing the right amount of data is not included as contributing to the path of mindfulness. As the behavioral and thought process associated with each of these steps is elaborated upon, it becomes clear that Buddhism is focused on the moral and spiritual dimensions of relationships as they are experienced in a constantly changing world. It is also clear that the Path requires a lifelong commitment, which differs radically from the short attention span and expectation of obtaining instantaneous results reinforced by cyberspace experiences. Perhaps more important in terms of the need to reduce the human impact on natural systems, the Path represents an alternative to the consumer-dependent lifestyle valued in the West. It is also important to note that different traditions of Buddhism are being taken seriously in the West, but not in sufficient numbers to have a real impact on the still growing influence of the digital revolution.

Confucianism, like Buddhism, is also a religion so deeply ingrained in daily cultural practices that it is understood more as the taken for granted reality of daily life. Its fivefold principles include the following: *Jen*, which "involves simultaneously a feeling of humanity toward others and respect for oneself, an indivisible sense of the dignity of life wherever it appears." *Chun tzu*, which highlights relationships that are the opposite of the competitive, petty, and ego-centered person. The person of Chun tzu puts others at ease and engages in what Martin Buber later referred to as I-Thou relationships and dialog. *Li* is the quality that leads to doing things correctly—in the use of language, in avoiding extremes, in the correct ordering of relationships within the family and society. *Te* is the power of moral example that attracts the willing support of the people. *Wen* refers to the "arts of peace," specifically the power of the arts to transform human nature in ennobling ways (Smith, 1991, 175–181). There is no mention of the importance of data in these life guiding principles. But the digital revolution, which is central to economic growth in China and other cultures with a Confucian past, is having a transformative impact on the youth of these cultures.

Given the emphasis on consumerism and the individually centered and Internet-connected lifestyles, it is doubtful that Confucianism will survive the pull of Western values. And given the levels of toxic chemicals dumped on the land and in the rivers, as well as the carbon dioxide being released into the atmosphere, Confucianism as a wisdom tradition may suffer the fate of other traditions that become overwhelmed by the glitze of consumerism and the illusion of freedom found on the Internet.

When we consider the older generation's Taoist emphasis on creative quietude, and its rejection of self-assertiveness and competition, it becomes easy to recognize how the digital culture, with its emphasis on change, commercialism, empowerment, objectivity, and entertainment, is a radically transforming force. The same holds for the Five Pillars of Islam that are more God-centered—and are promoted more systematically in schools and mosques. While the paths to mindful existence promoted by these religions, as well as by Judaism and Christianity, all focus on forms of consciousness that address the intentional nature of moral relationships, they are not being reinforced by the reality that is being digitized and that promotes consumer values. Nor have they overcome the internal and global forces leading to violence toward others.

Information about the history of religions, as well as their key beliefs, can be found on the Internet, just as all the information from books on indigenous wisdom traditions is available. But the personal experience of trying to reconcile the religious precepts with the conflicting social pressures cannot be digitally represented. Nor can the digital revolution lead to the inner transformations in consciousness and self-identity that would lead to adopting a life of voluntary simplicity—to cite just one example of a possible personal transformation.

The colonizing nature of the digital culture, with its cell phones, tablets, computers, and video games, brings about a change in consciousness and self-identity that aligns more with the Western values of seeking immediate gratification and material possessions, pursuing success in one's chosen career, ignoring environmental limits, and viewing the traditional knowledge and skills as sources of backwardness. That is, the digital culture does not enable people to experience the deepest levels of meaning and personal commitment previously associated with the wisdom traditions summarized here. But it can lead to the form of consciousness that reflects the adolescent stage of development promoted by corporate capitalism where everything is exciting, continually changing, free of long-term consequences, and seemingly in endless abundance.

As the media is largely owned by corporations that promote consumerism and a mix of libertarian/market liberal ideology we cannot expect them to contribute to the deep cultural transformations that the ecological crisis will force on us. Furthermore, with few exceptions our universities will continue to promote the silences and misconceptions that leave their graduates unable to recognize that technologies will not be able to solve the coming environmental cataclysm, and that there needs to be a sustained effort to reconstitute the deep cultural assumptions that underlie the industrial/consumer-dependent culture that is now being globalized in the name of progress and other Western values.

The seriousness of our failed educational systems, which includes both universities and public schools, can be seen in how few people are protesting the loss of privacy, their passiveness in the face of being hacked, their failure to question governmental authorities and political leaders who have put their ideological agendas ahead of addressing social justice issues, and their failure to recognize the importance of climate change. With computers now being viewed by most parents, teachers, professors, and politicians as the basis for major educational reforms, it is unlikely that there will be any sustained effort to alter how we will approach the end-game of collapsing natural systems.

One of the arguments being made against informing the public about the extent of the ecological crisis, including how few years we have to reduce its life-altering impacts, is that they will interpret the warnings as scare tactics and attack the messengers. Some critics have suggested that if the public is able to recognize that there are less draconian lifestyle alternatives they will then respond more constructively to the scientific reports about the changes we will face in the decades ahead. In the next chapter I will make the case for how to bring about cultural changes in ways of thinking and community-centered lifestyles. I have been writing for years about the nature of these changes, and how to bring them about. Given what was missing in the conceptual background of the audiences I attempted to reach—namely, that the ecological crisis is real and has its roots in the misconceptions and silences still perpetuated in education, the media, and the public they have influenced – the growing expressions of concern have still not addressed the misconceptions encoded in the language inherited from the past. Now that the extreme weather events are impacting people's lives in ways that should move them beyond denial—massive floods, tornados, extreme cold spells, droughts, and forest fires—perhaps my earlier common sense recommendations will be taken seriously.

That my total failure to initiate a discussion of critically important linguistic, cultural commons, and ecological intelligence issues at three Oregon Universities might be attributed to the fact that there is little visible evidence of climate change other than certain crops appearing weeks earlier than usual. Oregon still has adequate rainfall and the forest fires are in distant parts of the state. The daily experience of classroom teachers and university faculty is still largely unaffected by the environmental changes impacting other parts of the country. I suspect, however, that the reasons for ignoring the cultural roots of the ecological crisis go deeper, as there are faculty at all three of Oregon's major universities who are promoting discussions of environmental issues—but almost entirely from a scientific and technological solutions point of view. The deep cultural issues continue to be absent from their discussions, just as the issues were absent in their years of graduate studies with mentors whose thinking was based on the core assumptions that led to the first and now digital phase of the Industrial Revolution.

However, there are grounds for optimism even though it may be impossible to achieve within a few years what took feminists hundreds of years before people woke up to how language influenced consciousness and patriarchal cultural practices. The primary source for this optimism is the global spread of localism (or what represents more broadly the cultural commons) that is making the centuries-old patterns of abstract thinking and misconceptions learned in public schools and universities appear as irrelevant as the dissertations written by most of today's professors in the social sciences, humanities, and professional schools such as business and education.

7

LOCALISM, THE REVITALIZATION OF THE CULTURAL COMMONS, AND FACE-TO-FACE DEMOCRACY

Much of the turmoil in the West over the last 500 so years can in part be attributed to the abstract thinking fostered by an over-reliance upon the authority of print-based cultural storage, thinking, and communication. The religious wars that wracked Europe in the sixteenth and seventeenth centuries involved reducing the Other to abstractions that could be killed in the name of upholding a higher truth (which was also an abstraction), just as the Industrial Revolution relied upon a whole series of abstractions such as "worker," "profits," "markets," "technology," and "progress" to justify the exploitation of the children, women, and men who kept the machines running. As Steven T. Newcomb notes in *Pagans in the Promised Land: Decoding the Doctrine of Christian Discovery* (2008), both the Catholic Church and the American legal system relied upon a vocabulary of abstractions to dispossess the indigenous cultures of their land. Giving legal standing to such abstract metaphors as "heathens," "savages," "uncivilized," justified granting ownership to those who "discovered" and were "civilizing" the "New World." As discussed earlier, the vocabulary that justifies economic and technological globalization is also based on abstractions, such as rates of growth, value of currencies in relation to other currencies, amounts and value of natural resources, and the cost of production in various regions of the world.

Abstract thinking, which reduces the need for moral accountability in face-to-face relationships and with natural systems, also is the basis of the surveillance culture created by elites who have not considered the unintended consequences of their well-intended efforts—or perhaps they have decided to embrace them as a small price to pay for achieving more progress. The abstract world that lacks moral accountability has now been extended by the sub-culture of hackers and the anonymous producers of malware who are engaging in the early stages of cyber warfare, and by the reduction of people's performances and forms of knowledge to data and abstract information. Indeed, the disregard for the democratic process can be seen in how the digital and corporate culture have brought about profound changes in the world's cultures without seeking a vote of the people whose lives are being so irrevocably changed.

The assumption within the industry is that people now vote with their credit cards. Nearly every visual and printed representation of the happy consumer of the latest digital technology, as well as the ways in which the poor and homeless are accounted for, are also based on abstract thinking. There is so much cultural noise in the form of advertisements, ideologically driven media voices, information, data, television channels, and digital screens, that few people are able to recognize the life-altering changes occurring in their physical environments. Nor do they seem able to recognize the increasing threats to the credit card economy where cyber security experts now claim that 95 percent of all businesses in America have had their security systems breached. Instead of becoming aware of the life-altering changes due to the degradation of natural systems, the general mood of the majority of Americans is looking forward to when the growth of economy will accelerate even more. This, as the myth holds, will enable people to earn more money and thus move out of poverty and higher on the interconnected pyramids of consumerism and self-fulfillment.

The abstract thinking that in the past supported the further expansion of the global market systems has now reached the turning point where changes in natural systems, such as depleted fisheries, droughts affecting the price of food, shortages of potable water for growing food, and a momentary reprieve from a growing shortage of fossil sources of energy, point to the prospect of an even more dangerous future. The increasing number of armed conflicts and the growing attraction of joining extremist causes are in part the leading edge of the chaos that accompanies the loss of hope, cultural traditions, and the deepening poverty now experienced by a large segment of the world's population. As the West continues to promote a consumer-dependent lifestyle, the tensions and regional eruptions of violence will only spread. What constitutes the high status knowledge promoted in public schools and universities, which is increasingly being reduced to what can be processed by digital technologies and shared through online courses, cannot provide alternatives to these growing destructive global trends.

Abstract thinking has further degraded the democratic process as political scientists now focus on the distribution of votes and the economic and social forces that account for winners and losers. Students learn to think of the democratic process as a numbers game of red and blue states and of which party will control Congress. Learning about the historical roots of different ideologies, even when they are being misrepresented by the widespread Orwellian use of our political vocabulary, now is made irrelevant by the speed at with data can be digitally shared, analyzed, and used to predict winners and losers.

And what could be more destructive of the democratic process than the market liberal ideologically driven abstract thinking that led to the decision on the part of the Supreme Court to rule in Citizens United v. Federal Elections Commission that corporations and unions may spend freely on candidate elections? This, along with corporations already spending millions on lobbyists to guide favorable legislation through Congress and state legislatures, is turning an imperfect democracy into a plutocracy of the rich and powerful. Billionaires such as the Koch brothers, who possess a net worth of over 100 billion dollars, have shown a willingness to spend hundreds of millions of dollars to ensure the election of candidates whose thinking aligns with their libertarian/market liberal ideology. This ideology, which is part of the conceptual legacy of the Industrial Revolution, is in turn based on the abstract thinking of philosophers and social theorists who were unaware that the cultural assumptions they took for granted did not take account of environmental limits, and that the diminished life-sustaining capacity of the environment would be under further pressure from the majority of the seven-and-a-half billion people now seeking the basic necessities for sustaining life.

With both public schools and universities relying more upon digitally mediated learning, the abstract nature of print and data is further reinforcing a disregard of local cultural contexts, including the emergent and relational interactions within and between cultural and natural ecologies. Living as we do in cultural and natural ecologies involves multiple levels of information exchange that require being fully present in terms of relying upon all the senses and memory—including a well-developed awareness of being morally accountable and culturally informed about differences occurring in both the cultural and natural ecologies. Awareness of what is being communicated through the relational and emerging world is also dependent upon having acquired the language necessary for naming and thus making explicit the patterns of communication that otherwise go unnoticed. Few people demonstrate awareness that the digital revolution is driven by a libertarian/market liberal ideology that limits access to the place-based and intergenerational vocabularies necessary for becoming aware of essential information about the health of the cultural and natural ecologies upon which life depends.

The potential dangers of the growing data storage capacity of cloud computing, which is being rapidly expanded as corporations race to position themselves to take advantage of potential windfall profits, can be seen in the new Chinese Baidu cloud center that can store and process for various users the data equivalent of 268,000 Libraries of Congress (Mosco 2014, 34). Just as the abstract and ethnocentric theories of a small number of Western philosophers helped to put the world on a Titanic collision course with the environment, the scale of computing, and the abstract thinking it entails, is giving rise to a new elite class of data scientists who will "read" the data for correlations on which military, business, or police state strategy is most likely to succeed. Vincent Mosco summarizes how Big Data is changing our world: "We can now know the past, represent the present, and predict the future like never before, with little of this contaminated by flawed human decision making. The data will speak for themselves or through data-science magicians" (2014, 196). What this assumption overlooks is that the data is derived from watching people's lives, and it is always interpreted in terms of various users' ideological frameworks.

To recall how computer scientists, such as Hans Moravec and Ray Kurzweil, understand the historical forces that they view as dictating the technological progress requires the end of democracy. For them, the transition from face-to-face decision making within diverse cultural communities to cloud computing that serves environmentally and community destructive corporate and military interests is now beyond human control in the same way that Nature's logic of natural selection is beyond human control. Fortunately, many people are still capable of taking the first step in revitalizing local decision making, which is to be mindful that data provides only a surface and fragmentary account of a behavior and that it is ideology (that is, the abstractions of earlier thinkers) that turns the data into a living reality.

The Global Revitalization of Face-to-face Community-centered Alternatives to the Industrial and Now Digital Revolution

Humans now face a basic choice: In not questioning the modern myth of endless technological and economic progress Americans and much of the economic and technologically developed world continue living by this and other myths now accelerating the slide toward the sixth extinction as oceans become more acidic (predicated to reach a pH level of 7.8 by 2100) and climate changes lead to the loss of habitats that contributes to the loss of species (Kolbert, 2014, 120–124). There is, however, another choice that leads to a more optimistic view of the future; one that contributes to the revitalization of local democracy, to a reduced reliance on the more destructive consequences of the digital revolution, and to the recovery of awareness of how to live in face-to-face communities that are less dependent upon the industrial systems of production and consumption. These more sustainable ways of living continue to be followed by many indigenous cultures, and are being rediscovered by people in the developed world who, in taking the ecological crisis seriously, are recognizing the need to work together in communities that are less dependent upon the technologies and economic system now pushing the world toward a catastrophic ending.

These groups include educators promoting place-based education (Gruenwald and Smith, 2007), advocates of local agriculture (including urban agriculture) and transition towns, and the continued sharing of the largely non-monetized inter-generational knowledge and skills that even the promoters of the digital revolution unknowingly rely upon in their everyday lives. Collectively, they can be referred to as the cultural commons as the dominant values shared by these diverse approaches are rooted in face-to-face relationships and mutually suppor-tive patterns of living. Possessive and competitive individualism, the constant quest for new ideas, technologies, and personal material gain, are largely understood as the myths that sustained the environmentally and community destructive Industrial Revolution that has now entered its digital phase of globalization.

Also shared by these diverse and emergent social expressions of the cultural commons is the understanding of the need to change the old analogs that framed the meaning of words that fostered a taken for granted acceptance of the exploitation and suffering caused by the industrial/consumer/profit-oriented culture as the trade-offs necessary in order to achieve social progress (the lifting of all boats as Adam Smith put it—which is another abstract idea).

Just as the dominant belief system of each era had its own supporting vocabulary, such as the vocabulary of the feudal era where the individual was understood as a subject in a highly stratified world, the vocabulary of the industrial and now digital revolution where progress, profits, and data marginalized other ways of knowing, and the vocabulary of the cultural commons requires an ecologically and culturally informed reframing of the meaning of words such as "conservatism," "individualism," "intelligence," "wealth," and "poverty"—among others.

In an earlier book, *University Reform in an Era of Global Warming* (2011), I provide an extended discussion of how these and other currently used metaphors continue to reproduce the assumptions, misconceptions, and silences of earlier eras that ignored environmental limits and the dangers of hubris on the part of scientists and technologists. Here I will provide only a summary of the most salient changes necessary for aligning the reality-constructing metaphors with the dominant practices shared by the diversity of the world's cultural commons. Continued reliance upon the historically derived analogs that represented the individual as autonomous and competitive, wealth as measured in terms of the accumulation of money and power, and conservatism as promoting capitalism and limited government, would quickly lead to the integration of what remains of the cultural commons into the market system that is destroying the environment.

The basic move in analogic thinking, which involves understanding the new or revising the already familiar with ecologically and culturally informed analogs, is a form of comparative thinking or thinking of the new "as like" something already familiar. In the case of revising the analogs inherited from the past, such as those derived from the abstract thinking of Western philosophers, it involves using new understandings and experiences as the analogs for revising the meaning of words. One of the new understandings, at least for most Western thinkers, is based on the recognition that we live in constantly changing relationships, along with everything else that makes up the complex webs of interdependencies and information exchanges. These changing relationships and interdependencies, as discussed previously, are influenced by differences in cultural ways of knowing that are, in turn, influenced by the intergenerational experience of being long-term inhabitants of a bioregion. The important point to note is that overcoming the colonization of current thinking by outdated and wrongly constituted metaphors should not lead to reframing the meaning of words by relying upon other abstractions.

For example, while the Western idea of conservatism has a long history that continues to be ignored by people who now associate it with the liberal values of progress, free markets, and individualism, it's meaning can be rectified and aligned with the interdependent and largely non-monetized world of the cultural commons when the analogs are framed by an awareness of the need to conserve species, habitats, and the gift economy of intergenerational knowledge and skills practiced across a wide range of human activity. The heritage of what needs to be conserved and intergenerationally renewed includes the traditions underlying the arts, civil liberties, crafts, appropriate technologies, knowledge of the life cycles of the bioregion, as well as memory of wrongs done to others—including the non-human world.

While no one has ever observed an autonomous individual—that is, a person who does not exist in relationships with the built environment that encodes earlier forms of intelligence and aesthetic judgments, with other people, and the natural ecologies that are sources of oxygen, water, and protein—the idea of individual autonomy continues to underlie most of our cultural assumptions and moral norms. This metaphor needs to be reframed by recognizing that individual identity should include the ongoing relationships, behaviors, and values that guide these behaviors. Thus, there would be no fixed and isolated identity that leads to stereotypical thinking and to abstract universal rights such as private ownership of ideas and physical property. The use of nouns to refer to individuals and such supposed attributes as autonomy and intelligence, is what hides awareness of relationships and contexts. Instead, an ecologically and culturally informed understanding of individualism would be one where identity is emergent and judged in terms of patterns of moral reciprocity in an interdependent world of cultural and natural ecologies. In short, identities should reflect changes in relationships, and thus the impact of these relationships on other participants in the shared cultural and natural ecologies.

Similarly, intelligence is not limited to what is occurring in the human brain, but is encoded in the built environment, in the metaphorical language passed forward from generation to generation, and in the semiotic capacities of micro and macro ecological systems. The current understanding of intelligence, now heavily influenced by misconceptions carried forward in the field of cognitive science, still relies upon the assumption of the autonomous individual as the source of ideas, subjective feelings, and moral judgments. These misconceptions should not be passed over too lightly as they have important implications. For example, in *Blue Mind*, Wallace Nichols explains that the connecting pathways of the billions of neurons in the human brain produce every conscious and unconscious impulse, and "trigger the cascade of neurochemicals that mediate our emotions and behaviors in response to stress" (2014, 35). Excluded from this account are the multiple and diverse cultural influences that mediate emotions, how relationships will be interpreted, and what aspects of the emergent and relational world will be ignored.

As the cultural commons is a way of highlighting the importance of resisting the further degradation of natural systems by the industrial/market system of production and consumption, a revised understanding of intelligence needs to be consistent with what is unique about the non-exploitive examples of the cultural commons. Thus, the exercise of intelligence (to treat it as a noun is to turn it into an abstraction) should be understood as the ability to be aware of the emerging relationships and patterns of interdependence (that is, what is being communicated within and between cultural and natural ecological systems), and to adapt one's responses in ways that strengthen rather than undermine the patterns of mutual support. The exercise of ecological intelligence thus involves an awareness of how one's interpretation of the patterns that connect affects the mutual support systems within the cultural ecology as well as the life-supporting natural systems. When the educational process fails to provide the vocabulary necessary for making explicit the otherwise taken for granted cultural patterns, it is then limiting the ability to exercise the level of ecological intelligence essential to a sustainable future.

For example, the current meanings of wealth and poverty are two examples of how metaphors still reproduce the ecologically problematic assumptions of earlier eras in the West. The meaning of wealth in the developed West is still associated with the possession of money and political power, while the current meaning of poverty is largely associated with the lack of money and power. Within the context of the cultural commons, with its intergenerational gift economy essential to advances in the arts, crafts, healing practices, moral narratives, social justice traditions, and knowledge of local natural systems, the ecologically and culturally informed analog for reframing the meaning of wealth would be to associate it with possessing an in-depth knowledge of the traditions of the cultural commons and an ability to make a contribution to the community as a mentor, skilled craftsperson, artist, healer, and as a model of how to exercise ecological intelligence. The reframed meaning of poverty would be a lack of skills, knowledge, and moral insights that contributes to expanding people's symbolic worlds in ways that do not further degrade natural systems and the self-sufficiency of the community.

How Avoiding Lifestyles Based on the Culture of Print-based Abstractions Overcomes the Worst Abuses of the Digital Revolution, Restores Face-to-face Democracy, and Contributes to an Ecologically Sustainable Future

The earlier discussions of reducing the complex ecologies of everyday experience to what can be represented in print, or as data, provide the basis for an initial understanding of how much of daily life is now based on ideas, values, words, numbers, and visual images that encode the interpretative frameworks of strangers—who most often are represented as experts, social theorists, philosophers, economics professors, writers of computer programs, and so forth. The problem of living in ways dictated by the abstractions of others can also be understood in term of distances, which may take the form of the conceptual distance or degree of separation between the reality of what the printed word or data is supposed to represent and the lived experience of the individual. There is a huge distance or degree of separation between the Enlightenment philosophers who argued that traditions stand in the way of scientific and rational thought and today's reliance upon traditions such as the subject, verb, object pattern of English speakers, the ways in which metaphors carry forward previous ways of thinking, and the current understanding of private property, and so forth. The Enlightenment philosophers were perpetuating the West's traditions of print-based abstract and ethnocentric thinking and behaviors, just as the same patterns of abstract thinking of political theorists such as Ayn Rand and economists such as Milton Friedman now control the behaviors and economic policies of governments. The conceptual distance between Friedman's abstract theory of how free markets operate and the misery experienced by the unemployed impacted by governments that adopt his theory is often too great for people to recognize the source of the problem.

Helena Norberg-Hodge, the author of *Ancient Futures: Learning from Ladakh* (1991), head of the International Society for Ecology and Culture, and a leader in the localization food movement, made a number of important observations in her Tedx talk on the "Economy of Happiness" (now available on YouTube). One of the important points likely to be overlooked is that the local agriculture movement spreading around the world overcomes the problem of physical distances that are a major contributor to exploitive production systems such as the Foxconn factories in China that manufacture the components for Apple's high-end products. The globalization of industrial agriculture, in effect, also contributes to the problem of conceptual and moral distance (or abstract relationships) where there is less accountability for the exploitation of workers and the misuse of dangerous chemicals. To those who marvel at the advantages of modern technologies, having exotic fruits shipped in from thousands of miles away during the winter months is too often seen as yet another advantage of the technologically dependent age we live in. Yet it is the separation or distance that creates the abstract relationship between the producer and consumer, and marginalizes awareness of the moral and political issues that are becoming more important in our environmentally stressed world.

The distance between the decision makers in the corporate board room and the CEO's office about the need to increase profits by adopting more robots and computer-driven systems in the workplace, and the people who will be displaced is yet another example of how the primacy now given to abstract decision making leads to systemic social problems that seem on the surface to be unsolvable. The problem of distance between people's behaviors and the surveillance systems of corporations and governmental agencies should bring home to everyone how little accountability there is for those whose ideas, technologies, and economic policies impact the lives of others—all justified in high sounding words and phrases such as progress, national security, and development. The problem of conceptual distance between the corporate heads, politicians, and educators who made the decisions about the Common Core Curriculum, and the teachers and parents who must look on helplessly is yet another example of how much of daily life is governed by abstract systems and ideologies.

The degree to which everyday life for us as well as in other cultures is being regulated by abstract systems requires considering how pervasive print-based rules, explanations, and ideologies have become—as well as how data is now becoming the new basis of conceptual and moral authority governing decisions. Academics have a long history of discounting the importance of what is most distinctive about human life: namely, seeing, hearing, listening, remembering, imagining, feeling, loving, tasting, speaking, and being with Others where meanings are negotiated, and ambiguities and mysteries are never finally settled. The immediacy of these intersubjective experiences serves as the point of exchange in the information pathways that sustain the lived cultural ecologies. It was the drive to achieve equal standing with scientists that led academics to require that these verbs describing processes be turned into the fixed world of nouns. Subjectivity, or more correctly, the intersubjective combination of cultural/linguistic influences on the multiple dimensions of personal consciousness, is fundamentally misrepresented when reduced to fixed and objective accounts that can be printed in scholarly journals and in government documents announcing a new social policy.

As universities are now in a state of cultural lag and struggling to overcome the problem of academic disciplines that create artificial boundaries in a world of interdependent cultural and natural ecologies, it is time to focus on the different ways in which the cultural commons are being renewed as alternatives to the industrial system of production and consumption that is based on the abstract theories of earlier centuries and the hubris of today's scientists and technologists who do not have a deep knowledge of the cultures they impact in the name of progress.

All of the following examples of cultural commons activities involve face-to-face relationships and thus the moral accountability missing in the digital world of constant surveillance and sales promotion. The face-to-face world of the cultural commons also leads to place-based democratic decision making that is missing in the political process where a person's vote has little if any influence. The market liberal members of the Supreme Court have now ruled that billionaires and corporations have the constitutional right to buy the elections of candidates who will, in return, work to enact state and federal legislation that advances the interests of corporations and the wealthy elites.

The conceptual and physical distance between the individual's act of voting and the interplay of economic and ideologically driven forces over which she/he has no influence makes the national and even state-level democratic process little more than an empty ritual. Face-to-face democracy also has other advantages over the current system: namely, encountering neighbors and others in the community who have different points of view and interests yet are part of the network engaged in various activities of the cultural commons where inter-dependencies are more easily understood. These face-to-face relationships where the Other is not reduced to a political label lead to conversations and even arguments about the broader implications of the decisions that are to be the subject of a vote. Today's democratic process, where an individual's consciousness is under continuous assault from television attack adds, involves increasing isolation (conceptual distance) from others who may share common interests but differ on how to achieve them.

The increasing amount of time people spend on the Internet further increases this sense of separation—and thus the feeling that people who vote differently are the enemy. Face-to-face and place-based democracy overcomes the current tendency to transform the possibility of mutual exchanges on shared interests into abstract slogans and data on the percentage of votes for and against a specific issue or governmental policy.

The revitalization of cultural commons activities has other advantages missing in a world where people are being indoctrinated to identify their wellbeing with participating in the connected yet abstract world of the Internet. As pointed out earlier, the Internet has many advantages that are both personal and economic. And it is also essential to maintaining the complex systems that run the basic institutions and technological systems we now rely upon. Without the ability to measure and construct complex models of the behavior of natural systems there would be no understanding of the scale and rate of changes occurring in natural systems, and thus no real basis for recognizing the urgency of finding local cultural alternatives to the industrial system of production and consumption that undermines local economies that contribute to the self-sufficiency of communities.

As pointed out earlier, the digital revolution is also creating a new regime of truth, and this form of truth is based on the massive amounts of data collected and stored on people's lives. The myth of progress hides how this data is now being misused by corporations, and will be even more misused as people begin, in response to the deepening ecological crisis, to protest governmental policies and corporate practices. As people move from sit-ins and marches to taking more direct actions aimed at stopping the environmentally destructive practices of the utility and the energy extraction industries, as well as the corporations that reap huge profits from engineering and industrializing our sources of food and health care, the data now collected on people's lifestyles and patterns of thinking and associating with others will facilitate the country's transformation into a police state. As in the past, the police and National Guard have a poor record of supporting social justice movements, and they will continue to support the interests of the super-rich whose wealth is in maintaining the ecologically destructive economic systems.

Oracles of the digital future such as Eric Schmidt (Schmidt and Cohen, 2013, 81) claim that access to data will enable people to protect a democratic way of life. Unfortunately, they do not understand that the elites with a vested interest in the current economic systems and the high status forms of abstract knowledge are already exerting control over public schools (e.g., the common core curriculum and online courses). Nor do they recognize how data is used by the corporate-owned media (including the newspapers), and the role it plays in guiding election strategies at both the state and national levels. These elites also have at their disposal the context free metaphor of "terrorist" that can be used to label anyone who takes direct action against the corporations and super rich who are the real environmental terrorists.

The use of this metaphor will rally support for the use of police state measures from the vast majority of Americans whose educational backgrounds prevent them from recognizing further disruptions in the life-sustaining capacity of natural systems, such as a further increase in the acidification of the world's oceans and the killing off of predators such as sharks that play such an important role at the top of the food chain. In short, the myth of progress and its many genuine manifestations hides the basic reality that few want to acknowledge: namely, that the advocates of a police state could not have designed a more efficient system for suppressing any form of dissent.

The strengthening of face-to-face communities based on the intergenerational knowledge and skills of how to live less consumer-dependent lives will provide protection from the more destructive characteristics of the digital revolution. Face-to-face interactions related to various activities including the growing and sharing of food, healing practices, participating in the creative arts, engaging in making what is useful to others in the local community such as musical instruments and tools scaled to local use, playing games that no longer have to mirror the values of professional sports, and the sharing of intergenerational knowledge of how to avoid using poisons to control the environment, all involve a more limited reliance upon digital technologies. Face-to-face interactions will lead to less data being collected on relationships, including who might be sharing ideas with others that might be on a National Security or FBI watch list (which in the past included Martin Luther King, Jr.). Involvement with others in various cultural commons activities will also lead to a less rushed lifestyle that will reduce the need to become part of the Internet of Everything culture where every aspect of the household, including a person's clothes and physical changes, will be wirelessly monitored, regulated by sensors, and communicated to experts. Greater reliance upon barter systems, use of local currencies, and the simple act of volunteering also means that a person's personal life is not adding to a data profile that governments and corporations now rely upon to track, predict, and guide people's behaviors.

Other key points in Norberg-Hodges' Tedx talk included the following: (1) That the local movement in the growing and sharing of food leads to more opportunities for people to work and thus earn a living (which does not happen with industrial agriculture); (2) That it contributes to biodiversity (which is undermined by genetically engineered and corporate-controlled large-scale agriculture); (3) That small farms lead to the production of more food (a point supported by the recent announcement by the UN that industrial agriculture should be terminated); (4) That the real divide is not between the right and left, but between local and global approaches to agriculture.

Local approaches to agriculture also exhibit the best characteristics of the intergenerationally connected face-to-face cultural commons. That is, local knowledge of the interconnections between weather patterns, types of soil, and varieties of plants—as well as recipes and how to preserve different foods—is passed forward in face-to-face conversations that strengthen a sense of mutual interest and thus community. These conversations are also about past experiences within the community that lead to unanticipated problems as well as how the community came together in solving them—which might have been about the misuse of water resources or other environmental miscalculations. These face-to-face conversations, which also extend to sharing information about family activities and challenges, also strengthen the sense of being part of a larger cultural and natural ecology that has a history—which carries with it the prospects of a shared future. Included in some cultural commons are the prejudices and exploitive practices handed down over many generations, but the face-to-face relationships can be more effective in changing attitudes than writing about social justice reforms—especially when the people perpetuating them are not likely to be readers. Again, the element of conceptual distance becomes a factor in holding people to be morally accountable. It is important to note that collecting data on who associates with whom, as well as surveillance of the trail left by the use of credit cards, and other abstract systems of misrepresentation, are noticeably absent in cultural commons relationships and activities.

The increasing number of farmer's markets held across the country, which have doubled in size over the last two years, is an example of what is best about the cultural commons. People representing the diversity of the community—in terms of skills, ethnicity, religions, and personal life histories—share their stories, concerns, and model the values that strengthen the bonds of community. These same community-strengthening characteristics of local markets exist in other countries, and they have few of the impersonal and exploitive characteristics of shopping malls or the isolated nature of the consumer experience on the Internet.

Other expressions of the revitalization of the cultural commons include the informal networks of creative people ranging from local theater groups, to musicians, writers, and craftspersons. The latter, for example, combine working with their hands, reliance upon the knowledge of a craft accumulated over many decades, and a heightened sense of aesthetic judgment to create out of wood, fibers, and other materials gathered from the natural environment both beautiful and useful objects for the community. These networks, as well as the networks of other creative groups in the community, are in their own way ecologies of interdependent relationships, diverse skills, and wealth exchange systems where money plays a less central role.

If a survey were to be done on who represents the mentors in every community that carry forward the depth of intergenerational knowledge and skill passed forward and intergenerationally renewed and expanded upon, we would find that this gift economy has other benefits such as people experiencing better physical and psychological health. The cultural commons also represents the wide range of community-centered possibilities for the increasing number of people who are being replaced by the new wave of digital technologies, and who may discover that engaging in cultural commons activities reduces what previously was assumed to be the level of income necessary for sustaining life.

Millions of American men and women who are losing traditional jobs and are drifting to the lower-paying service jobs that rob them of their sense of dignity and of possessing a real skill are sitting on the sidelines of the consumer culture. They are often depressed, and feeling trapped in a system over which their previous education limits their sense of control. The question not being raised is how many would find hope and a renewed sense of purpose if they had learned about the cultural commons and acquired the skills and talents to become participating members? By limiting their education in ways that prepared them for work in a technologically driven and market-oriented system, rather than in a more balanced program that included the arts and the skills that contribute to the self-sufficiency of the community, they are being denied the possibility of acquiring the form of wealth that strengthens self-respect as a contributing member of a community. It is also important to note that this form of wealth cannot be taxed and thus cannot be used to support the industrial/military complex now committed to perpetual warfare.

What sets these cultural commons networks apart from the consumer lifestyle now increasingly dependent upon the abstract world of the Internet and the industrial system of production is that being engaged in growing food, performing in the arts, learning about the life cycle of species in the local environment, and so forth, provides the best insights into what needs to be conserved and intergenerationally renewed. Shopping online and in shopping malls provides no basis for recognizing that the production process may be based on the exploitation of workers that mirrors the early days of the satanic mills of the English Midlands, and that the natural materials used in the manufacture of the consumer item so artfully displayed are increasingly limited. There is nothing that communicates about the need to conserve the gift resources and economy of the natural world.

As nearly every cultural commons activity is dependent upon knowledge and skills passed forward through mentoring and face-to-face relationships, there is a clearer understanding of the importance of traditions—including traditions based on earlier misconceptions and prejudices that need to be reformed. The community-enhancing traditions, or what should be understood as the gift economy of the cultural commons—that is, the wealth that strengthens communities and leads to personal discoveries and development of talents—are not what is represented in textbooks or a printed text read on a computer screen.

Print-based accounts of traditions are useful but too often turn into abstractions for the reader, which are easily displaced by other abstractions that appear more exciting and personally relevant. Those who make the case that the knowledge, techniques, and practical uses of traditions can be found on the Internet simply have no understanding of the ecology of information, tacit patterns of reinforcement and modeling of skills, and the emotional/moral development of personal identity that accompanies face-to-face relationships. This, of course, should not be taken to mean that all face-to-face relationships, and the intergenerational knowledge being passed forward, are free of oppressive relationships and ecologically destructive ideas and values. The intergenerational knowledge and values passed forward by those socialized to take for granted the deep cultural assumptions that underlie the progressive nature of an industrial and consumer-driven culture continue to contribute to the downward spiral we are now witnessing in both natural and cultural ecological systems.

When we take account of the network of interdependent relationships within the cultural commons, we find what is widely missing in the sham democratic process where people are told they must vote according to their personal economic and other interests, but in a rigged system where corporate and private wealth determines the outcome of elections at the state and federal levels. That is, the miseducation in public schools and universities, as well as through the corporate-controlled media, that emphasizes that voters act politically on their self-interest, is now being challenged by street demonstrations and Internet resistant groups (which work for both the right and left). What is missing, as demonstrated by the recent Occupy Movement, is an awareness of the traditions being overturned by the computer scientists, corporations, and technological devotees. This lack of awareness can be seen in the widespread failure of the public to demand that the culture-changing technologies—such as the surveillances systems, replacement of workers with computer systems, the militarization of local police (only now being questioned), the introduction of the Internet of Everything, the increased reliance on cloud computing, and the ways in which the digital revolution is being used to colonize other cultures—be subject to the democratic process. The silence suggests that people's lives have become so hurried and on the edge of just surviving economically that they lack the free time necessary to reflect on what is being lost. It also suggests that they have uncritically accepted the Enlightenment ideology passed forward in public school and university classrooms as well as through the corporate-controlled media that represents traditions as impediments to progress.

What is being widely overlooked is Shils' warning that once a tradition is lost it cannot be recovered. For those educated to think that every effort to address the ecological/cultural crises we now face should be criticized, they need to consider how we can restore the old traditions of privacy so central to our legal protection, or restore the traditions of craft knowledge and the expectation of being able to earn a living as computer systems displace the need for workers.

It is questionable whether the growing support of the localization movement will engage more than a small minority of the world's billions of people, and whether it will provide a non-violent transition to a more sharing, equitable, and intergenerationally connected future. Also to be taken seriously is the question some scientists are raising about whether humans as a species are capable of redirecting their evolutionary development in ways that are less dependent upon consumerism and the conveniences of modern technologies in time to avert the collapse of the life-sustaining ecological systems. Both questions lead to confronting the existential question of how to live in the face of these uncertainties. Should we pursue the lifestyle dictated by the modern assumptions about individual self-realization and the secular trinity of scientific, technological, and capitalism-based progress promoted in public schools and universities?

Those who are not consciously taking responsibility for ensuring the prospects of future generations, as well as not discovering their own talents and sources of meaning in the mutually supportive networks of their cultural commons, are likely to find that these questions, in being unanswerable in terms of hard data, serve as an excuse for continuing their hyper-consumer lifestyle. Yet awareness that fundamental environmental changes are occurring has stimulated a wide range of thinking that challenges the old taken for granted daily patterns that are in addition to the localization movements mentioned above. These include finding alternatives to the old sources of consumer dependencies. These range from the expanding sharing economy which seems less driven by an awareness of environmental limits to groups deeply aware of the necessity of creating ecologically sustainable alternatives to the existing industrial and environmentally exploitive system that still controls the popular images of what constitutes personal success and our national destiny of leading the world into the supposedly new digital era.

These groups include the Business Alliance for Local Living Economies that represent what Jerry Mander refers to as hybrid capitalism (2012). BALLE is the organizational hub of a network of small community-centered businesses that are focused on local hiring, production of local products and services, and worker participation in decision making and even ownership, and using the profits to strengthen local communities. The network, which also includes locally owned banks that support the ecologically informed values of the BALLE movement, includes over 20,000 small businesses spread across the United States and Canada.

Other groups promoting alternative community-centered lifestyles include the Schumacher Center for a New Economy which has as its agenda the following: support of local economies, sharing the commons, ownership by workers, regional currencies, sustainable production and consumption, appropriate technologies, and responsive government. The transition communities (Hopkins, 2008) that have sprung up in England and are now being adopted in other parts of the world, are also important examples of community-wide efforts to become self-sufficient in terms of food, sources of energy, local currencies, and thus politics. The goal of the transition communities is to drop out of the over-500-year industrial diversion from the traditional path of human dependence upon the cultural and natural commons.

The deep cultural assumptions that underlie the efforts of the computer scientists, corporations, and consumer and technological devotees to transform the world into one governed by super computers are noticeably missing from the thinking of people who participate in the local networks that carry forward the various forms of cultural commons knowledge and skills. It is not that they do not use cell phones, read books, and rely upon the Internet for information; rather, these technologies are used more for the purpose of advancing mutually supportive activities and relationships. They have no transformative vision of a globally digitally connected and change-oriented world. In short they have no colonizing motivation and vision for changing others. Rather their focus is on carrying forward and improving upon traditions that strengthen community in ways that represent alternatives to the consumer-dependent lifestyle that is increasingly leading to poverty and powerlessness. It is also important to recognize that the cultural commons of ethnic groups are similarly focused on carrying forward the traditions essential to their identities and core values as well as enabling their members to contribute to their communities. In many instances they are also connected by the Internet to others working to sustain their cultural commons from being overwhelmed by the appeal that the digital revolution has to their youth. But they also lack the hubris and messianic drive of those promoting the digital revolution that raises such important questions about what the future holds, given that the super-rich and powerful elites are not likely to give up peacefully the myths that have guided the industrial and now digital revolution.

The other important observation that needs to be made is that public schools and universities continue to reinforce the surface knowledge that is reproduced in print and now data, as well as the myths about objective knowledge and the cultural neutral nature of science and technology. The silences in the thinking of computer scientists, the army of consumers of the latest digital technologies, and the corporations in need of new profit-producing products can in part be attributed to the failure of teachers and faculty who continue to reproduce the deep cultural misconceptions and silences they learned during their graduate years of study. Cultural lag is real, and the consequences of being socialized to accept abstract thinking as the basis for promoting technologies that do not take account of the cultural traditions into which they are introduced will lead to endless conflict as the decline in life supporting ecosystems accelerates.

An example of how many educated Americans have been conditioned by an uncritical reliance on the authority of print to be abstract thinkers, and thus to ignore the ethnographic evidence of people's behaviors, can be seen in the claim that the cultural commons only exist in rural (and the culturally backward) areas and among indigenous cultures. This stereotypical and thus abstract pattern of thinking ignores the many ways that urban areas are vital centers of cultural commons activities. Yet this pattern of thinking has destructive consequences. I have encountered arguments from highly educated people (one an editor of an important journal) that we cannot go back to an earlier lifestyle as well as the claim that the cultural commons attracts too few people to have a positive influence in addressing the ecological crisis. This is also an ideologically driven way of thinking that will prevent people from asking the most fundamental questions about the range of intergenerationally connected activities and relationships that have not been monetized and that have a smaller adverse ecological footprint. Sometimes it is the seemingly obvious and boldest statements that turn people away from exploring what lies behind and beyond the world of abstract pronouncements.

To reiterate two key points: computer scientists do not possess a knowledge of the cultures into which their technologies are introduced—which is also a characteristic of the consumers who eagerly embrace each new innovation even though the long-range view of the computer scientists is to replace most human activities with robots and computer systems. The second point that should be the focus of a public debate is whether the introduction of new technologies, such as the Internet of Everything, cloud computing, and the replacement of workers by robots and computer-driven systems, should be subject to a democratic vote—which would require creating forums that engage the public in in-depth discussions of the importance of the traditions that will be overturned by the new technologies as well as who gains and who loses. This is where the question raised by some scientists about whether the human species has the capacity to redirect its evolutionary development becomes important. The control that the language inherited from the past exerts over current thinking, and the economic stakes associated with how this linguistic inheritance privileges a few over the many, reminds us to consider how many hundreds of years it took the feminists to reframe the analogs that sustained a patriarchal world view that still exists in many parts of the world. Can computer scientists, their supporters, and the general public begin to recognize the linguistic roots of the colonizing trajectory the world is now on? I have serious doubts, but what are the existential alternatives to challenging the silences by reminding people that the heritage of intergenerational knowledge and skills that sustains the local cultural commons may hold out the best prospects for the future of their children?

BIBLIOGRAPHY

Angwin, J. 2014. *Dragnet Nation: A Quest for Privacy, Security, and Freedom in a World of Relentless Surveillance*. New York: Times Books.

Bateson, G. 1972. *Steps to an Ecology of Mind*. New York: Ballantine.

Berger, P. and T. Luckmann. 1966. *The Social Construction of Reality*. New York: Anchor Press.

Bowers, C. 2000. *Let Them Eat Data: How Computers Affect Education, Cultural Diversity, and the Prospects of Ecological Sustainability*. Athens: University of Georgia Press.

Bowers, C. 2011. *Perspectives on the Ideas of Gregory Bateson, Ecological Intelligence, and Educational Reforms*. Eugene, OR: Eco-Justice Press.

Bowers, C. 2011. *University Reform in an Era of Global Warming*. Eugene, OR: Eco-Justice Press.

Bowers, C. 2012. *The Way Forward: Educational Reforms that Focus on the Cultural Commons and the Linguistic Roots of the Ecological/Cultural Crises*. Eugene, OR: Eco-Justice Press.

Bowers, C. 2013. *In the Grip of the Past: Educational Reforms that Address What Should be Changed and What Should be Conserved*. Eugene, OR: Eco Justice Press.

Bowers, C. 2014. *The False Promises of the Digital Revolution: How Computers are Changing Education, Work, and International Development in Ways that are Ecologically Unsustainable*. New York: Peter Lang.

Brynjolfsson, E. and A. McAfee 2013. *The Second Machine Age: Work, Progress, and Prosperity in a Time of Brilliant Technologies*. New York: W. W. Norton.

Carr, N. 2011. *The Shallows: What the Internet is Doing to Our Brains*. New York: W. W. Norton.

CRCIS. (n.d.). "About us" Retrieved from http://noorsoft.org/fa/aboutus, accessed October 23, 2015.

Dawkins, R. 2006. *The God Delusion*. New York: Bantam Books.

Diamandis, P. and S. Kotler. 2012. *Abundance: The Future is Better than You Think*. New York: Free Press.

Drexler, K. 2013. *Radical Abundance: How a Revolution in Nanotechnology Will Change Civilization*. New York: Public Affairs.

Dyson, G. 1998. *Darwin Among the Machines: The Evolution of Global Intelligence*. New York: Basic Books.

Dyson, G. 2012. *Turing's Cathedral: The Origins of the Digital Universe*. New York: Penguin Books.

Easterly, W. 2013. *The Tyranny of Experts: Economists, Dictators, and the Forgotten Rights of the Poor*. New York: Basic Books.

Ellul, J. 1964. *The Technological Society*. New York: Vintage.

Geertz, C. 1973. *The Interpretation of Cultures*. New York: Basic Books.

Goody, J. 1977. *The Domestication of the Savage Mind*. Cambridge: Cambridge University Press.

Gruenwald, D. and G. Smith (eds). 2007. *Place-Based Education in the Global Age: Local Diversity*. New York: Routledge.

Hacker, J. and P. Pierson. 2010. *Winner-Take-All Politics: How Washington Made the Rich Richer – and Turned Its Back on the Middle Class*. New York: Simon & Schuster.

Hamshahri Online. June 26, 2006. "New technologies: Threat or opportunity?" Retrieved from www.hamshahrionline.ir/details/653, accessed October 23, 2015.

Havelock, E. 1986. *The Muse Learns to Write: Reflections on Orality and Literacy from Antiquity to the Present*. New Haven, CT: Yale University Press.

Hayek, F. 1944. *The Road to Serfdom*. Chicago, IL: University of Chicago Press.

Hoffmeyer, J. 2008. *A Legacy for Living Systems. Gregory Bateson as Precursor to Biosemiotics*. Dordrecht: Springer.

Hopkins, R. 2008. *The Transition Handbook: From Oil Dependency to Local Resilience*. Totnes: Green Books.

Huesemann, M. and J. Huesemann. 2013. *Techno-Fix: Why Technology Won't Save Us or the Environment*. Gabriola Island: New Society Press.

Idhe, D. 1979. *Technics and Praxis*. Dordrecht: D. Reidel Publishing.

Intergovernmental Panel on Climate Change. Report No. 5. www.ipcc.ch, accessed October 23, 2015.

Ishizawa, J., and G. Rengifo. 2011. "Revitalizing the Ecological Intelligence of Andean Amazonian Communities: The Way Back to Respect." In Bowers, C. *Perspectives on the Ideas of Gregory Bateson: Ecological Intelligence, and Educational Reforms*. Eugene, OR: Eco-Justice Press, pp. 163–184.

ITDM. 2012. "Convention." Retrieved from http://itdm.ir/misagh.php, accessed on October 23, 2015.

Joy, B. 2000. "Why the Future Doesn't Need Us." *Wired*, April.

Kayhan. May 5, 2014. "Virtual colonization, a serious threat to family privacy." Retrieved from http://kayhan.ir/fa/news/12018, accessed October 23, 2015.

Kolbert, E. 2014. *The Sixth Extinction: An Unnatual History*. New York: Henry Holt and Company.

Kurzweil, R. 1999. *The Age of Spiritual Machines: When Computers Exceed Human Intelligence*. New York: Viking.

Kurzweil, R. 2005. *The Singularity is Near: When Humans Transcend Biology*. New York: Viking.

Kurzweil, R. 2012. *How to Create a Mind: The Secret of Human Thought Revealed*. New York: Viking.

Lakoff, G. and M. Johnson. 1980. *Metaphors We Live By*. Chicago, IL: University of Chicago Press.

Lakoff, G. and M. Johnson. 1999. *Philosophy in the Flesh: The Embodied Mind and Its Challenge to Western Thought*. New York: Basic Books.

Mander, J. 2012. *The Capitalism Papers: Fatal Flaws of an Obsolete System*. Berkeley, CA: Counterpoint Press.

Mayer-Schonberger, V. and K. Cukier. 2013. *Big Data: A Revolution that will Transform How We Live, Work, and Think*. New York: Houghton-Mifflin.

McChesney, R. 2013. *Digital Disconnect: How Capitalism is Turning the Internet Against Democracy*. New York: The New Press.

Moravec, H. 1990. *Mind Children: The Future of Robot and Human Intelligence*. Cambridge, MA: Harvard University Press.

Moravec, H. 2000. *Robot: Mere Machine to Transcendent Mind*. New York: Oxford University Press.

Morozov, E. 2013. *To Save Everything, Click Here*. New York: Public Affairs.

Mosco, V. 2014. *To the Cloud: Big Data in a Turbulent World*. Boulder, CO: Paradigm Publishers.

Muehlhauser, L. 2013. *Facing the Intelligence Explosion*. Berkeley, CA: MIRI.

Newcomb, S. 2008. *Pagans in the Promised Land: Decoding the Doctrine of Christian Discovery*. Golden, CO: Fulcrum Publishing.

Nichols, W. 2014. *Blue Mind: The Surprising Science that Shows How Being Near, In, or Under Water can Make You Happier, Healthier, More Connected, and Better at What You do*. New York: Little, Brown.

Nisbett, R. 2003. *The Geography of Thought: How Asians and Westerners Think Differently … and Why*. New York: Free Press.

Norberg-Hodge, H. 1991. *Ancient Futures: Learning from Ladakh*. San Francisco, CA: Sierra Club Books.

Office of the President of the Islamic Republic of Iran. May 13, 2014. Full text of the speech of the President at the Fourth National Festival of Information and Communication Technology. Retrieved from http://president.ir/fa/82322, accessed October 23, 2015.

Ong, W. 1982. *Orality and Literacy: The Technologizing of the Word*. New York: Methuen Publishers.

Putnam, R. and R. Leonardi. 1993. *Making Democracy Work: Civil Traditons in Modern Italy*. Princeton, NJ: University of Princeton Press.

Rand, A. 1961. *The Virtue of Selfishness*. New York: Signet.

Reddy, M. 1979. "The Conduit Metaphor—A Case of Frame Conflict in Our Language About Language." In Andrew Ortony (ed.), *Metaphor and Thought*. Cambridge: Cambridge University Press, pp. 284–323.

Ross, R. 2009. *Returning to the Teachings: Exploring Aboriginal Justice*. Toronto: Penguin Books.

Roszak, T. 1986. *The Cult of Information*. Berkeley: University of California Press.

Schmidt, E. and J. Cohen. 2013. *The New Digital Age: Reshaping the Future of People, Nations, and Business*. New York: Alfred A. Knopf.

Shabecoff, P. and A. Shabecoff. 2008. *Poisoned Profits: The Toxic Assault on Our Children*. New York: Random House.

Shils, E. 1981. *Tradition*. Chicago, IL: University of Chicago Press.

Shiva, V. 2005. *Earth Democracy: Justice, Sustainability and Peace*. Cambridge, MA: South End Press.

Smith, H. 1991. *The World's Religions*. New York: Harper One.

Spretnak, C. 2011. *Relational Reality: New Discoveries of Interrelatedness that are Transforming the World*. Topsham, ME: Green Horizon Books.

Stock, G. 1993. *Metaman: The Merging of Humans and Machines into a Global Superorganism.* New York: Doubleday.

Suzuki, D. and P. Knudtson. 1992. *Wisdom of the Elders: Honoring Sacred Native Visions of Nature.* New York: Bantam Books.

Tabnak. June 6, 2012. "The Internet, an opportunity or a threat?" Retrieved from www.tabnak.ir/fa/news/249474, accessed on October 23, 2015.

Turkle, S. 2012. *Alone Together: Why We Expect More from Technology and Less from Each Other.* New York: Basic Books.

Whitehead, A. 2010. *Process and Reality.* New York: Simon and Schuster.

Wilson, E. 1998. *Consilience: The Unity of Knowledge.* New York: Alfred A. Knopf.

Winner, L. 1977. *Autonomous Technology: Technics-out-of-Control as a Theme in Political Thought.* Boston, MA: M.I.T. Press.

Winner, L. 1986. *The Whale and the Reactor: A Search for Limits in an Age of High Technology.* Chicago, IL: University of Chicago Press.

INDEX

virtual reality 51, 54–5, 63
vocabulary 14, 27–34, 61, 63–4, 68;
  connectivity 71; localism 76–8, 80, 82

Wald, G. 71
warfare 66, 76, 88
water shortages 10
wearable technology 12, 35
West 1–4, 6–7, 9–11, 13–14, 16;
  colonization 35–8, 40, 42, 44;
  connectivity 60, 63, 67–9, 71–4, 77;
  construction of reality 28; data cults 18,

21, 23; language misconceptions 26,
  30–2; localism 76–8, 80–3; Muslim
  cultures 46–9, 51–6; tradition 24
Wikipedia 9, 68
Wilson, E.O. 1, 14, 19, 64
Wintun culture 70
wisdom traditions 62–75
World War II 28, 38

Yarralin culture 69
YouTube 83